Social Commerce & MarTech

THE FUTURE OF WORK

Social Commerce & MarTech

JOANNA HUTCHINS

Marshall Cavendish
Business

Published in 2023 by Marshall Cavendish Business
An imprint of Marshall Cavendish International

A member of the
Times Publishing Group

Other Marshall Cavendish Offices:
Marshall Cavendish Corporation, 800 Westchester Ave, Suite N-641, Rye Brook,
NY 10573, USA • Marshall Cavendish International (Thailand) Co Ltd, 253 Asoke,
16th Floor, Sukhumvit 21 Road, Klongtoey Nua, Wattana, Bangkok 10110, Thailand
• Marshall Cavendish (Malaysia) Sdn Bhd, Times Subang, Lot 46, Subang Hi-Tech
Industrial Park, Batu Tiga, 40000 Shah Alam, Selangor Darul Ehsan, Malaysia

Marshall Cavendish is a registered trademark of Times Publishing Limited

ISBN 978-981-5113-82-2

Printed in Singapore

Contents

WELCOME TO THE FUTURE OF WORK

In today's digital age, social media has become an integral part of our lives, from sharing photos and staying in touch with friends to discovering new products and services. But what if social media could do more than just connect us with others? What if it could also revolutionise the way we shop? This is Social Commerce.

This revelatory book delves into the cutting-edge innovations at the convergence of social media, technology and the marketplace. To survive and thrive, businesses are finding ingenious ways to leverage technology to deliver more personalised, relevant, and engaging experiences for customers, while also respecting their privacy and data rights. From shoppable posts to virtual influencers to AI-powered consumer insights, social commerce is poised to be a key frontier for MarTech (marketing technology), and a critical success factor for the brands of the future.

The Future of Work is a game-changing collection of business books that explore the rapidly evolving landscape of work today. Within the next five years, many jobs will disappear, many will be created, but what is certain is that all will change. The titles in this new series, written by some of the most influential business leaders, thought leaders, practitioners and consultants in the industry, cover everything from business trends and technological innovations, to revolutions in work culture and the critical skills you'll need in order to stay ahead of the curve.

Chapter 1

Introduction

MARKETING IS IN THE MIDST OF A TECHNOLOGY-FUELLED RENAISSANCE

Having been in marketing for nearly 30 years, today it feels like a more daring and exciting field than ever before. The dazzling array of AdTech, MarTech and BrandTech innovations are unparalleled in industry history and are generating a renaissance within marketing, advertising, and branding. From programmatic media buying to Direct-to-Consumer (DTC) brands that rely exclusively on social media marketing, to generative AI for images and copywriting to click-to-buy social commerce, there has never been a more exhilarating time to be in marketing.

By contrast, in the 1990s, when I was first starting my career in advertising on Madison Avenue in New York, it was pre-internet, pre-digital revolution. Only a few CEOs had mobile phones, which were the size of a briefcase. No one had computers on their desks. Memos were dictated to secretaries who would then type them up and physically distribute or fax them. Presentations were not in PowerPoint, they were delivered orally by brand managers and advertising executives based on memory and supported by visual aids that took days or weeks to create, like hand-drawn illustrations of product prototypes or storyboards. TV and print shoots would take weeks and months, with teams often having to decamp to Los Angeles for six weeks for post-production, as only Hollywood editors had the special effects skills needed for final TV commercial cuts.

At that time, there were databases of consumer information that were updated quarterly or annually – which made us feel magically all-knowing, as we could monitor what magazines and newspapers people were reading and what latest TV shows they were watching. The most exciting part was that we could sta- tistically cross-tabulate the target audience with hobbies and interests and magically identify their favourite shows and thus know where exactly to advertise. Brands were spending hun- dreds of millions of dollars on 30-second and 60-second TV advertising, using the all-important sandwich structure: demon- strate the consumer problem in a lifestyle setting to attract the desired audience, introduce the product that solves said prob- lem, and then wrap up with a happy customer bathing in the glow of the product benefits and a problem solved. This struc- ture was called a sandwich because the product was the meat at the centre. While TV commercials probably annoyed some view- ers, the only way to skip them was to leave the room during the commercial break.

Advertising and marketing were gloriously creative but, as you can see, messy and imprecise. Brands used to joke that they knew that half their advertising was highly effective, they just wished they knew which half! When the internet, email and soft- ware came into play, it was agreed that the industry had made significant leaps forward in how to communicate more efficiently and showcase ideas. But were websites and email necessarily closer to the consumer? They were just new channels for messaging delivery.

Contrast that with today's targeted marketing, where the consumer journey is increasingly frictionless, where an ad viewed on social media can lead to a single click to purchase, with the item delivered to the consumer's doorstep in a matter of days, if not hours. In this new ecosystem of marketing, every click is captured, brands know exactly who the consumer is, what they respond to that leads to purchase; all this purchasing data is geolocated and available real-time, enabling hyper-localized targeting. Marketing has shifted into the realm of performance marketing, with marketers knowing exactly how to engage consumers and capture likes and leads, and then move the engagement to a one-on-one marketing experience to convert to sales.

This is why today, I personally leap out of bed everyday with an enthusiasm I have not felt since my early days on Madison Avenue in New York. If the fundamental premise of marketing is to connect with potential customers about a product or service and build relevancy and connection with an intent to make a sale, then today's world of tech-driven marketing can do that with more accuracy, precision, and efficiency than ever before.

TECHNOLOGY IS TRANSFORMING MARKETING POSSIBILITIES AND OUTCOMES

While technology continues to rapidly evolve, it has already transformed the lives of marketers and consumers. The availability of information today is unparalleled. This makes it easier than ever for consumers to access information about products, services and brands, and has led to a shift to a more discerning, informed and empowered consumer who is more likely to research and compare products before making a purchase. On the brand side of the equation, brands know their consumers better than ever before and can better develop products and services that solve needs and problems and improve people's lives every day.

Further, advances in technology and data have enabled more personalized experiences. By leveraging data to understand consumers, even niche segments, brands can create targeted messaging and personalized offers that resonate deeply with their consumers. This is better for consumers as well as brands – both sides can cut through the clutter more easily and find one another.

Overall, digital marketing itself means that consumers and brands are interacting continuously. Communication is now a two-way street. As a result, brands must be more proactive in building relationships with consumers and providing exceptional customer service and experiences. And consumers hold them accountable for this, calling them out if they do not live up to their promises. Engagement with most brands is now not only frictionless but also ever-present across email, social media, search engines, websites, and mobile apps, all of which have transformed access and engagement.

And as social media gives rise to influencers and creators, social platforms have become even more valuable to brands beyond paid advertising. The individual influencers and creators who have built large followings on social media platforms have established a level of trust and credibility with their audience. Given their intimacy with their followers, they are often more accessible, authentic and influential than other forms of advertising and promotion. In addition to promoting products or services to generate awareness and buzz, they also help shape consumer behaviour and influence purchase decisions. Based on their deep understanding of their followers' tastes and interests, they are used by many brands as incubators and creators for new product development and innovation.

Finally, the data that these systems generate means that as brands have access to nearly unlimited insight, they are able to engage in real-time decision making. This immediacy of information has led to an agility in marketing that has never before been possible. From a brand operations point of view, you can metaphorically drive the car as you are building it, making data-driven decisions and responding with very little to no lag time between consumer action and brand reaction. When this is repeated on an infinite feedback loop, marketing gets exponentially smarter and more efficient.

With technology now evolving more rapidly than has been seen in any lifetime, groundbreaking innovations are announced so frequently that it seems as if there is something industry-changing being launched on a weekly basis. From social commerce and livestreaming selling, to generative AI large language platforms like ChatGPT and text-to-image AI platforms like Midjourney, technology continues to transform and automate the brand and marketing world. And we are just at the beginning.

So where do we focus when our heads are turned by the next dazzling array of tools? Let's start by digging into one of the most rapidly growing segments: social selling and social commerce.

Chapter 2

Social Commerce & Frictionless Purchasing

While social commerce feels like a brand-new idea, many would argue that social commerce in its most basic sense has already been around more than 20 years on Amazon, Ebay, or even Craigslist. Indeed, the concept can be traced back to the early days of e-commerce, when businesses started using e-commerce platforms with social aspects such as communities of people coming together to buy and sell goods, leave comments and reviews, and make recommendations. The first known use of the term "social commerce" was in 2005 by Yahoo! in a blog post by employee Steve Rubel, where it was defined as the intersection of social networking and e-commerce. Since then, social commerce has evolved into a more specific definition and has come to be understood as buying directly on a social platform without having to migrate to another platform or website to complete the purchase. Today, social commerce essentially integrates social media with the functionality of e-commerce to allow customers to make purchases directly "in app" within their social media channels or through referral links.

Social commerce has taken off in recent years due to the growing use of social media overall, the rise of influencer marketing, and the desire for a more seamless online shopping experience. Its growth is not surprising as it represents a win-win for both businesses and consumers. The benefit to brands is enormous in that it allows them to reach their target audiences directly; meanwhile, it benefits consumers by enabling them to seamlessly discover and purchase products without leaving their social media apps, creating a buying experience that satisfies consumers' demand for frictionless shopping and purchasing. On top of that, it is interactive, exciting, and often feels a lot more like entertainment and a lot less like promotion from brands.

Social commerce takes many forms, including in-feed shoppable posts, social media marketplaces, and social shopping apps. Essentially, it is a way for businesses to leverage the power of social media to not only build brand awareness but also drive sales at a higher rate of conversion due to the ease of purchasing. In 2021, the global social commerce market generated around US$724bn in revenue, and it has been projected to grow at a compound annual growth rate (CAGR) of 30.8% between 2022 and 2030.[1] This growth is driven by the increasing number of internet and social media users, rising e-commerce sales, and the growing adoption of mobile devices globally.

The Asia-Pacific region is the largest market for social commerce, accounting for more than 40% of the global market share, due to the high population density, increasing smartphone penetration, and growing e-commerce sales in countries such as China, Japan and South Korea.

North America and Europe are also significant markets for social commerce, with the US and UK being the largest contributors in these regions.

CHINA AS A WINDOW INTO THE GLOBAL FUTURE OF SOCIAL COMMERCE

China is widely regarded as the pioneer of social commerce, with social commerce having been in play since around 2016, whereas in other large markets in 2023 it is still nascent. Today, it is flourishing in China and accelerating at a pace not seen elsewhere in the world. Social commerce is expected to reach $475bn in sales by the end of 2023, constituting more than 14% of China's total e-commerce sales – more than 15 times the size of social commerce sales in the US.[2] This disproportionate growth can be attributed to a unique business model that utilizes "enabling innovations" for a truly frictionless buying experience. Specifically, by leveraging existing innovations such as e-commerce functionality, livestreaming sales and group buying, and bolting them onto social, Chinese tech companies have created an entirely new and intoxicating entertainment and shopping universe – one that is at once social and shoppable.

In the West, social commerce is at its core a *supply-driven model* that exists on a social network[3] – a network where friends connect with one another and where brands and sellers have a platform to deploy an advertising business model to push product information and content to shape buying decisions of potential consumers. Also critically important is the social component, where buyers share their purchases in their social feed, drawing attention organically to the brands and products. The purchase process itself, however, can be cumbersome as it typically happens on an external website, which requires the prospective buyer to take a series of additional steps – they must click through from the social network to the website, potentially navigate the website to find the desired item, add the item to their cart, enter their shipping, billing and payment details, and finally click to buy. This leads to a high proportion of "shopping cart abandonment" at various stages of the purchase process.

Conversely, Chinese social commerce has innovated the model to be a *demand model* within a social group.[4] Social commerce apps gather consumer but do not rely on individual networking or connections as their starting point. The apps' primary draw for users is informative, entertaining thematic content geared towards certain target audiences and their interests, e.g., fashion and beauty, news and information, etc. This also happens to capture a focused and high-potential group of pre-qualified consumers to brands and sellers. Individuals who join the app can connect with each other, or not, but the experience is enhanced through social connections. The enabling innovation here is embedding e-commerce into social and activating it with dynamic functionality such as livestreaming sales. Importantly, purchasing is typically completed in the app itself, taking as few as two actions – tap to select the desired item, tap to authorize in-app payment, all done! While there is advertising in the app, the business model is dominated by commissions from e-commerce sales that are supercharged by livestreaming selling events hosted by celebrities and influencers. Brands in China have achieved conversion rates of almost 30% on social platforms, which is almost ten times higher than conversion in the conventional e-commerce world.[5]

THE LANDSCAPE OF SOCIAL COMMERCE IN CHINA

China's development in social commerce can be traced back to the early 2000s, which saw the rise of social media platforms like Renren and Kaixin001. However, it was not until the emergence of WeChat that social commerce started to build momentum as the WeChat platform added Mini-Programs in 2016 and public accounts started to become popular channels for marketing and shopping. The rise of social commerce in China has further developed with increasing consumer expectations for personalized and interactive shopping experiences, which is now satisfied by a variety of platforms like WeChat, Douyin (TikTok), and Xiaohongshu (Little Red Book).

As of 2022, WeChat has over 1 billion monthly active users and has become a one-stop shop for many Chinese consumers, offering features such as messaging, mobile payment, and Mini-Programs for shopping and services. Douyin has over 600 million daily active users, and its short-form video format has become an effective way for brands to showcase their products and engage with consumers. Xiaohongshu is a popular social commerce platform among young, urban, affluent Chinese consumers, offering a range of curated content dominated by beauty and fashion themes. All platforms offer fully functional social commerce with direct purchasing in app. Their race to provide increasingly frictionless experiences to capture more of the consumer spend has resulted in a highly competitive market. As a result, if we study the landscape of social commerce in China – which is easily 10 years ahead of the rest of the world and progressing at a much faster rate of technological development – we can most likely predict the future of social commerce in other markets. So, let's mine the China market for insights into social commerce for the rest of the world.

THE WORLD'S MOST VALUABLE UNICORN AND VISIONARY IN SOCIAL COMMERCE

You may have never heard of ByteDance, but you most certainly have heard of its breakthrough product, TikTok. Today, Beijing-based ByteDance is the most valuable startup unicorn in the world, after only 10 years of operation. Valued at over US$350bn[6] at the end of 2021, with 110,000 employees (double the staff of Facebook)[7] and 1.9bn monthly active users across 150 countries and 75 languages[8], ByteDance operates the most popular news app in China, Toutiao (Today's Headlines), as well as the global sensation short-video social sharing app TikTok, known as Douyin in China. TikTok/Douyin alone has been downloaded 3.3bn times globally,[9] comparable in downloads to the entire Meta group of global companies including Facebook, Instagram and WhatsApp. ByteDance's founder Zhang Yiming's fortune doubled in 2021 to reach over US$59bn, and this with only 22% ownership of ByteDance, making him the second-richest man in China.[10]

Unlike the Alibaba conglomerate that dominates the e-commerce landscape in China, ByteDance has become a global business phenomenon as the first Chinese technology company to experience breakout success worldwide, which was achieved at a speed that has left the global tech industry reeling. Sheryl Sandberg, formerly COO of Meta Platforms, expressed competitive concerns over TikTok during her tenure as COO, stating, "They're growing really quickly, they've gotten to bigger numbers faster than we ever did."[11] In fact, in 2022, stocks of Meta Platforms crashed by more than 40%, with industry analysts suggesting that TikTok's success was to blame for Meta's poor performance.[12]

The core enabling innovation of ByteDance is its proprietary technology stack of artificial intelligence (AI) recommendation algorithms and user profiles, which are combined to deliver highly personalized content. This is markedly different from other social apps, which have historically relied on search or social connections' likes as the main method for users to self-select content. Instead, ByteDance's apps feed the user personalized content based on a user profile that is generated from user data, so the more the user engages with the app, the smarter the algorithm gets, and the more personalized and relevant the content becomes. This is what makes the TikTok user experience stickier and stickier – some might say even addictive. This technology stack is a breakthrough that no competitor has yet to match with anything approaching the same results. Facebook tried with Lasso, a TikTok-inspired app, piloted in Mexico in 2018, but Lasso failed and was off the market by 2020, with fewer than 80,000 daily active users.[13]

The irony is that the founder of TikTok does not see the platform as a social app at all, even though this is how the world characterizes it. Rather, Zhang believes TikTok is a content-based community and often comments that the app is more of a short-video TV platform for the modern mobile age, as opposed to a video-first social media platform. It is no surprise, then, that the orientation of the technology stack is about linking users with content that they will enjoy. The social component is secondary to the content as the driving feature, but it just so happens that other users, with similar profiles and interests can and do connect. However, the user feed is ultimately highly personalized based on the individual user profile in the app, and what users see is not driven by their social connections' likes and comments. And, of course, a great deal of this content and the feed is heavily branded. Do you like that eye makeup or those sneakers? In one click you can buy them.

Yet this technology was not initially developed for TikTok. It emerged in one of ByteDance's first products, Toutiao, a daily news and information aggregator app in China – an unlikely source for a content-to-commerce platform. Toutiao was one of the company's first products and was based on insights Zhang gathered from his past experiences. Prior to Toutiao, ByteDance – which at the time was approximately 30 people working in a Beijing apartment – had launched a number of smaller apps in the entertainment space, mainly based on memes. None were particularly successful, but with every failure, Zhang accumulated important learnings about what worked, what did not, and what users' pain points were. Prior to ByteDance, Zhang had worked in a number of Beijing-based startups, such as 99fang (real estate app) and Kuxun (travel app), as well as established stalwart Microsoft. Based on these experiences, he recognized a set of three unmet needs and pain points that no platform had successfully solved:

1. The small screen of a smartphone and the resulting limitations for mobile browsing;

2. Users' fragmented time, such that the moments when they wanted to browse – a few minutes in a queue or waiting for the bus – were so short as to limit their ability to engage with typical content formats; and

3. Information overload of news, entertainment and social, such that it was not easy for individual users to navigate to the content most relevant to them.[14]

Zhang decided to solve these needs using a news and information platform, on the basis that news is something that people look at even if they only have a minute, because staying informed is a basic human need. But he also wanted to go one step further and design a platform that could best serve its users, using big data and machine learning to make highly personalized recommendations.

At the time, in 2012, using AI to curate news was a radical concept. News was a business where information was curated by human editors – it was individuals who decided which stories were "big" and which were not. The original news platform and the model for all others was the Yahoo! portal. But in fact, this model was merely the existing news model overlaid on the technology of the internet. It fundamentally failed to leverage the power of the channel. News was not personalized other than if a user indicated they preferred to see world news over local news, or sports over business. For users, most news was still search-based – if they wanted to read about a current event, they often searched for it on Yahoo! or Google, or if they were in China, they used the search engine Baidu. Zhang envisioned a product that would shift this dynamic. Instead of people looking for information, information would look for people. By moving from search to recommendation, he would remove the need for the user to take specific action. Spotting this opportunity was the key to Zhang disrupting the news and information industry by leveraging the under-utilized power of the channel to serve users better, providing a customized product that delivered greater convenience and better outcomes.

Toutiao's user profiles are its key to hyper-personalization. It comprises three types of data[15] that Zhang felt would most accurately capture the information needed to deliver highly relevant content to each user. First, there is user data, including demographic information like age and gender, as well as type of device, browsing history, etc. Second, content data is gathered, which includes the typical catalogue of content the user engages with. Third is environment data, such as where the user is, the stability of their network, home versus workplace, whether they are on public transport, what the weather is like at their location.

Toutiao then applies machine learning to anticipate user tastes. Two key processes are used: (1) content-based filtering, which offers recommendations to users based on past content viewed; and (2) collaborative filtering, which builds group profiles of users who enjoy similar types of content and uses one user as a proxy to select the content served to the others.[16] Content is then optimized based on what the user might like to read, which gives the content a "recommendation value" score. Likes, click-throughs and completion rate increase recommendation value, while short reading time decreases it. Recommendation value also decreases over time as information goes out of date. With every click or hover, the data network effect takes over; as the algorithm gets smarter, the user profile becomes more robust, understanding more and more what content users prefer. With a better user experience, users are more engaged spending more time in the app, which further enriches the user profile, which creates even better content matching, and so on.

With 45% user retention rates[17] in Toutiao in 2012, one of the highest ever seen globally at that time, Zhang knew he was on to something big. By creating the filtering processes and user profiles and combining them, Zhang had successfully innovated an AI-driven growth flywheel that set a new standard for personalization and could be an engine for any type of user platform and a game-changing technology disruptor for ByteDance.

With this flywheel, Zhang realized that ByteDance could become an app factory. All they needed to do was identify unique app concepts with a supporting content model and apply the content-plus-personalization flywheel. And further, as apps go in and out of fashion, it did not matter if some failed, because the information generated by the technology stack could still be used to enrich user profiles and improve the recommendation engine across all apps, making current and potential new apps stickier and stickier. This kind of sticky platform powered by a personalization flywheel would be a boon for advertisers and brands to reach their target consumers.

Finally, Zhang believed this flywheel transcended culture, which would give him the opportunity to explore a global super app – a feat never before achieved by a Chinese company. With 80% of the world's internet users outside of China,[18] the biggest opportunities were in overseas markets. But successful global apps typically relied on some cultural adaptation and human curation when moving overseas, which had prevented many Chinese apps from becoming global, with the fixed cost of product development for new markets being high. But Zhang felt his growth flywheel reduced the need for large-scale adaptation and human curation, as with AI as the engine, the user profiles themselves acted to naturally adapt the app, so the cost of serving an incremental user for ByteDance would be close to zero.

This realization led to Zhang breaking off several teams from the main business to experiment with what these new global apps could be. These teams enjoyed the resources of the larger business, for example engineering, programming and legal support, but they were relieved of profit and ROI pressures or seeking investment – which gave them an advantage over other external, independent startups who had to balance both financing and development. Under this operating structure, the teams were encouraged to undertake systematic experimentation to find the world's next super app. Zhang felt that a news and information app from China could be too politically sensitive, so Toutiao was not going to be the candidate for becoming a global super app; instead, he had a sense that there could be something in the space of entertainment.

They finally hit gold a couple of years later by exploring learnings from the still successful and growing Toutiao. In 2015, with Toutiao having revolutionized the news and information game in China, overall content on the internet and apps had also evolved globally thanks to smartphones and 4G connectivity becoming prevalent, with short-form video emerging as a new, highly engaging form of content. On Toutiao, Zhang observed that short video content (6–15 seconds long) was stickier than any other content. He wondered if this could lead to a new platform for ByteDance. He also saw new short-video, music-driven platforms like Vine (US), Musical.ly (China-based, with users in US and EU) and Kuaishou (China) taking off with young, trendy users. So, he tasked an incubation team of 10 employees (from the now 2,000-strong business of Toutiao) to explore short-form video, giving them the simple brief to explore "mobile TV for the world"[19] using the ByteDance flywheel. Douyin/TikTok was born from this incubator and soon launched across China and Japan.

Ironically, in China, digital marketing and e-commerce were not as developed as in the US then. In the US, tech startups scaled their platforms by relying on sizable, data-driven sales and digital marketing budgets to spread the word and acquire users. Douyin focused instead on lower-cost and more viral ways of acquiring users – mainly in building content which would be at the centre of pop culture and pull users into the app because of its trendiness. They engaged China's urban youth by sponsoring a hip hop talent show, "The Rap of China", which also was able to generate free high-value short-video content for the app. In China as well as globally, Douyin/TikTok set up challenges to give users not only the motivation to produce content, but also a framework to make content creation simple. The challenges often went viral, spreading beyond Douyin and taking over social media globally. It didn't take long for brands to tag onto this trend to leverage the virality of the content.

By Q1 2018, Douyin/TikTok was the world's most downloaded app,[20] and by 2020 it enjoyed the highest retention rates in China in the industry at close to 90%.[21] There were even people on YouTube creating videos *about* TikTok videos, with many of these being 10 minutes long and garnering millions of views themselves. To create "a Douyin" or "a TikTok" became common parlance in the internet world for creating a short video. Douyin/TikTok was taking over the culture of the internet.

A concurrent challenge was how to monetize the app as user momentum was building. One such tool for monetization, inspired by computer gaming, was in-app purchases of virtual coins. Users could buy TikTok Coins with real money and buy things in the app like emojis as well as "gifts" or "diamonds" to give to their favourite content creators as tips in appreciation for the content. If the creator wishes to cash in their gifts or diamonds for real money, the app takes 50% of this as commission. From June 2018 to May 2020, the platform experienced 4,233% revenue growth in in-app purchases, and in 2022 revenue was estimated to be US$78m.[22]

Advertising is by far the largest contributor to the platform's revenue. Using the same personalization engine as for content, TikTok/Douyin delivers extremely targeted messages, which has made it the go-to app for digital marketing and advertisers like the NBA, Coca Cola, The Washington Post, Apple, BMW and Marvel, to name just a few. It has become the main revenue engine for the app and is such a popular channel for social selling that Douyin/TikTok was estimated to constitute 5.3% of the total global digital ad market at US$31.66bn in sales in 2022.[23] Nearly 40% of the company's employees were sales staff in 2019,[24] with this staff not only selling ad space but advising advertisers on content. Advertising often looks like – and to some degree is – another form of content, taking the shape of video challenges, entertaining content and hashtags that go viral. This type of advertising content performs better than other channels for advertisers as it is more enjoyable and thus more watched by the target audience than the traditional product-presentation advertising. And by adding e-commerce buying functionality, where users can buy items they see in the videos, Douyin/TikTok essentially pioneered a new social selling tool, now known as social commerce. In its first year alone, total sales from social commerce were US$119bn, and by 2022 this was estimated to increase to US$180bn, a growth of 35%.[25]

AGRICULTURE JOINS THE DIGITAL REVOLUTION WITH SOCIAL COMMERCE

Founded in 2015, Pinduoduo is the Chinese e-commerce Goliath that you have likely never heard of. Pinduoduo is an agriculture-focused digital platform and app that connects 16m farmers directly to consumers. It is the fastest-growing e-commerce business in China's history, achieving unicorn status two years after its launch, eclipsing the rise of Alibaba's Taobao, which took five years to achieve the same.

Agriculture, in any economy in the world, has the lowest rate of digitalization – yet the products are fundamental to our daily lives. This innovative platform enabled farmers to participate in the fast-growing digital economy in China, widened access to consumers, and generated both greater sales and profits by going direct to the consumer. Consumers, of which there are 741m monthly active users,[26] get access to more variety and better prices thanks to the reduction in the complexity of distributors, supply chain and logistics, all of which typically take their cut along the way.

The Pinduoduo app has a simple, easy-to-use interface specifically designed for those with limited digital app experience. It works on an easy-to-shoot, edit and upload format, where merchants can showcase the farms and the produce – from the story of the farm and the growing conditions to incredibly detailed photos and information on the produce itself, like how to use it in cooking or even DIY beauty recipes like avocado facial masks. Consumers can buy household-sized quantities of produce to arrive at their homes, fresh from the farm, in 1-3 days' time. Since the platform launched, it has expanded beyond produce to include other branded daily staple goods as well.

The platform leverages the power of social by enabling users to "pin" an item to their social media feed, inviting their social connections to join in a group buy with highly advantageous group pricing. Prices for group buys (with groups sometimes as small as three people) can be 50–75% lower than the usual price – a big win for the app's consumers who are more price-conscious than brand-conscious. Consumers have 24 hours to assemble a group buy, bringing a high sense of urgency and irresistible gamification to the buying experience. With the group sharing and buying component, Pinduoduo has achieved an unheard-of customer acquisition cost of $2 per customer, compared to $41 for Taobao.[27] Livestreaming sales further enhance the experience for both sellers and users. Finally, buyers are incentivized with rewards toward future purchases to post photo reviews of their purchases on the seller's page, enhancing the credibility of the seller and the engagement of the buyer. All this user engagement has led to a 7-day retention rate of 77%, the highest of any e-commerce platform in China.[28]

Pinduoduo has generated massive value creation by assembling existing social, e-commerce, and group buying practices and combining them in a simplified and easy-to-use format that enables a population of farmers and rural consumers, often without internet and relying only on cellular data services, to join the digital revolution. Unlike other e-commerce in China, Pinduoduo taps into an underserved group that are not already buying these products online. Pinduoduo users tend to be in lower-tier cities or in rural communities and skew older, lower-income, lower-education, and female[29] (in these homes, females are typically in charge of managing the household purchasing). In doing so, Pinduoduo has helped to improve the lives of these communities by providing access to better prices and fresher products, and has been lucrative for both the farmers selling on the app and the platform itself. In 2018, Pinduoduo listed on the NASDAQ at a valuation of $20–24bn. In 2022, Pinduoduo's market capitalization was nearly $60bn, making it the 280th most valuable company in the world.[30]

A CONTENT-TO-COMMERCE INNOVATOR IN BEAUTY AND FASHION

The fastest-growing social commerce app in China is Xiaohongshu, created for young women 18 to 35 years old, focused on fashion, beauty, and lifestyle. Founded in 2013, its name means "little red book", but it is also known in English as RED. Xiaohongshu describes itself as a lifestyle sharing platform; it can be thought of as Instagram meets Pinterest meets Amazon – a social, shoppable, video-led content platform fed with user-generated content.

Xiaohongshu has earned a reputation for cultivating an experience known as "growing grass" (*zhongcao*)[31], a Chinese internet colloquialism referring to the FOMO (fear of missing out) sensation of seeing a product owned by others and wanting it too. Growing grass has been lucrative. As of November 2021, Xiaohongshu was valued at US$20bn, with 300m registered users and 100m monthly active users.[32] For a frame of reference, this valuation puts Xiaohongshu at roughly the same size as Heineken or Toyota globally.[33]

The content on Xiaohongshu is a mix of captivating images that seem to spring from the pages of a fashion magazine alongside dynamic and addictive short-video content from users and brands alike – with frictionless integration from content to purchase, creating an irresistible shopping experience for users. The most lucrative format for generating sales has been livestreaming, which is part of what Xiaohongshu calls its "content to commerce"[34] system, an enabling innovation bundle that allows brands to directly connect and manage their marketing and selling relationships with consumers. Highly engaging and interactive, the livestreaming commerce feature leverages the closed loop from "online sharing" to "community interaction" which promotes brands and their products and builds a bridge to consumption – with high conversion and repurchase rates, high customer orders, and low product return rates.[35] Global luxury brands such as Louis Vuitton, Givenchy, Gucci and Tiffany find the affluent Gen Z female demographic of Xiaohongshu so compelling, they clamour for prime livestreaming slots.

SHOULD WE BE FAST-FOLLOWERS OF CHINESE SOCIAL COMMERCE?

It's essential to note that the Chinese e-commerce and social commerce landscape is unique and may differ significantly from other regions. Also, China as a country and nation of consumers has earned a well-deserved reputation for being an early and rapid adopter of new technologies and trends; social commerce is no exception. With Chinese platforms and brands easily 10 years ahead in this space versus the rest of the world, China can be viewed as a lens with which to peer into the future of social commerce and likely other yet unimagined consumer, social and shopping innovations. This is why brands and businesses can and should stay abreast of, study, and extrapolate learnings from the innovative approaches and practices that have been successful in the Chinese market to stay ahead of the curve in other regions.

Chapter 3

Branding in a Social-Enabled DTC World

In the last two decades, consumer brands have experienced a period of consolidation, with large companies getting larger and consolidating product categories and brands through growth and/or acquisition. Global behemoths like P&G, Nestlé, Unilever and L'Oréal have bought some the world's favourite indie brands, filling the gaps in their portfolios for homemade, natural brands and products. For example, Unilever acquired quirky, socially responsible Ben and Jerry's ice cream in 2000 and L'Oréal acquired the ethically responsible beauty brand The Body Shop in 2006. These acquisitions took place quietly, however, against a global backdrop of growing consumer sentiment that big companies were getting too big. Skeptics shared suspicions that once acquired, these quality brands would be cost-reduced and streamlined into mass market submission, rendering them no more special than the ordinary mass market brands that they sat alongside in the corporate portfolio.

It is no surprise, then, that the trend in the last five years has been an evolution in the model of consumer brands, facilitated by the internet age. No longer are new businesses reliant on getting a spot on supermarket or drugstore shelves, which comes at a great cost due to retailer slotting fees. Nor are they constrained by the weighty capital required to open their own brand retail stores. With the growth of e-commerce, brands and businesses can go direct to the consumer without the need to sell into retail buyers or to build up expensive distribution chains. Direct-to-consumer (DTC) brands have blossomed, with *Inc.* magazine reporting upwards of 400 being launched as of 2018.[36] The ability of DTC brands to disrupt large multinational incumbents in their industries has attracted billions of dollars in venture capital investment. These brands are digitally native, much faster-moving than their so-called "fast moving consumer goods" counterparts, and with the conventional retail element removed, they have an even closer proximity to the consumer – every business and brand's goal.

For these brands and companies, social media provides a valuable forum for consumer insight and data gathering. Whether it is simply social listening to gather consumer sentiment on hot topics or brands, analyzing influencers and user-generated content for trending product insights, or data mining to extract valuable information on consumer browsing, interests and purchasing behaviour, social platforms are fertile ground for businesses to identify consumer patterns and trends to base their products and marketing upon.

In fact, social media is such fertile ground that some entrepreneurs have built entirely new brands and offers based on social insights and trends and sold exclusively on social commerce, skipping "traditional" e-commerce altogether. This is a fascinating value chain in that it has the potential to further refine and develop the DTC business model. In this social media and social commerce model, we see a dramatic compression in time and costs to get to market.

What might the future of socially generated and operated brands look like? China has the world's largest online population, with over 1.15bn internet users and 900m active social media users.[37] This vast user base generates a staggering amount of consumer data. However, it is worth noting that there are strict regulations around data privacy in China, some of the strictest in the world – extending well beyond Europe's General Data Protection Regulation (GDPR) legislation. So while the data is vast, it is not beyond the scope of consumer data available from social in other countries; therefore the learnings from China on leveraging social are in fact widely applicable anywhere in the world.

One key element we see in Chinese businesses is that they rise to the top by knowing their consumers more intimately than their competition. Social platforms, whether social media or social commerce, bring businesses closer to the consumer and enable this intimacy. By understanding consumers' needs and wants better, businesses can define and deliver a value proposition that is highly relevant and irresistibly attractive to the consumer. And even beyond that, these businesses are not only able to engage with their consumers more directly and more deeply on social media but are also able to continually surprise and delight them with innovation that addresses unmet needs based on these insights. It is a positive and upward spiral of value exchange between both company and consumer, resulting in a win-win outcome. This depth of understanding and engagement also generally results in greater consumer retention and repur-chase rates. And we know that loyal consumers often become advocates, which results in a low- to no-cost word-of-mouth lead generation and conversion channel for sales.

A DISRUPTIVE BEAUTY BUSINESS BUILT ON AND BY SOCIAL MEDIA AND SOCIAL COMMERCE

In November 2020, after four years of eye-popping growth, Chinese beauty unicorn Yatsen Group made history as China's first beauty brand to go public, launching its offering on the New York Stock Exchange. The company's multiple beauty brands – some of their own creation and others acquired – had become the #1 selling brands online in China's fast-growing e-commerce market. Founded in 2016, Yatsen Group is the creation of Proctor & Gamble (P&G) alum and Harvard Business School graduate, Jinfeng (David) Huang.

While at P&G in the market research department, Huang noticed that the market leaders were all foreign. L'Oréal, Estée Lauder, LVMH and P&G dominated the Chinese beauty market. Further, he observed they were all competing rather conventionally – using high-cost television advertising and high-profile celebrities to build brand awareness while focusing on physical retail and beauty advisors for product recommendations and ultimately making the sale. While this had been an effective path to growth historically, he spotted a potential gap that he believed could not only be filled by a local Chinese brand but might also disrupt the entire industry in China. Seeing where China was headed in terms of digital and e-commerce and how younger Chinese consumers and beauty enthusiasts were starting to get heavily engaged in social media platforms like Xiaohongshu, Huang saw an opportunity for a beauty company that behaved differently from the international players and was more tech-savvy, better reflected local consumer preferences, and overall was more responsive to local consumer needs.

In fact, the rising generation of Millennial and Gen Z Chinese consumers were more likely to embrace new local brands, which were untarnished by the quality scandals of previous generations. They felt proud to buy and use Chinese brands. Not only that, consumers also had complaints about foreign beauty brands. Specifically in colour cosmetics, many Asian consumers struggled to navigate the colour palettes that were not designed for Asian skin tones, failing to provide the necessary colour range. Using social listening research, it was observed that many younger consumers found international brands confusing and shared the sentiment that "Chinese brands know what is good for local consumers".[38]

Fresh from school with an MBA from Harvard, Huang formed the Yatsen Group. Yatsen was named as such because it was the name of Huang's undergraduate university, Sun Yat Sen, which was in turn named after the first President of the Republic of China. Like Sun Yat Sen, Huang felt this company would also represent a new possibility for China – a Chinese-born beauty brand for Chinese consumers, born from social and directly addressing consumers' needs. Huang's ambition was to unseat the market leaders in colour cosmetics at the time – L'Oréal, LVMH and Estée Lauder held a combined 47.8% market share[39] – and to do so with a completely different approach to the market. He intended to combine his knowledge of the beauty business with his understanding of the digital ecosystems of China to create a business model that was a fusion of beauty and social media-enabled tech to disrupt the industry.

Yatsen Group's first move was to create three different colour cosmetic brands. With colour cosmetics being largely fashion- and trend-based, Huang felt there was too much risk in having just one brand and that a portfolio of brands would mitigate risk in case one or two of the brands were underperforming at any given time. The first brand created was Perfect Diary, a colour cosmetic brand targeting Millennials and Gen Z with a slogan of "unlimited beauty". The slogan represented the value proposition, which was good quality at attractive prices, enabling consumers to buy many colours, play and experiment. The business started online, primarily selling through Alibaba's Taobao and TMall channels and later launching sales on social platforms including Xiaohongshu, TikTok/Douyin, and WeChat through the Mini-Programs function. Perfect Diary was a major success, being the first domestic colour cosmetic brand on the infamous 11.11 shopping day to hit RMB100m (US$14.1m) in sales on TMall in 2018.[40] Within five years, largely based on the success of Perfect Diary and its position as the number one domestic cosmetic brand in China, Yatsen Group conducted an IPO on the NYSE with a valuation of US$4.46bn.[41]

So how specifically did Yatsen Group leverage social media-enabled tech to disrupt the industry and build a unicorn beauty business in China? Unlike their foreign competitors with large R&D and marketing teams, the Perfect Diary staff is dominated by data scientists and programmers. They have built an artificial intelligence (AI) and data-driven business which keeps getting smarter and smarter and is fuelled by social media platforms and insights.

Perfect Diary harnessed the power of China's Key Opinion Leaders (KOLs) with large followings on social media. There are over 3m KOLs in China, so many that there is a 5-tier ranking system on the basis of how many followers each KOL maintains. The top-tier KOLs have more than 5m followers, the middle tier 300,000 to 1m followers, and the lowest tier less than 100,000 followers. Perfect Diary saw a role for all tiers and developed its internal team and database to measure the performance of each of their 15,000 KOLs.[42] The system measured various KPIs, including number of followers, number of active followers, post views, number of likes or favourites on posts, number of comments, number of forwards or shares, and more. The aggregate analysis resulted in a content engagement score, which was used to evaluate each KOL's impact for the brand. This was then input into a model that linked the KOLs to brand sales. The outcome of this was more effective utilization of KOLs, resulting in stronger ROI for KOLs for Perfect Diary versus other competitors.

Perfect Diary managed the KOLs closely, providing content guidelines and co-creating content with them. For example, they chose four specific KOLs whose appearance and personality were well suited to Perfect Diary's four Animal Eyeshadow Palettes, with each representing a different palette that best suited them – resulting in more than 200,000 of the palettes being sold in a single week.[43]

Perfect Diary also used KOLs to develop new product innovations. As Huang explained, "When we develop a new product, we send samples to 1,000 to 2,000 KOLs to try it. Maybe 50% to 60% of KOLs like it and are willing to promote it to their fans and tell them that Perfect Diary is planning to launch this new and exciting product. But at this time consumers cannot buy it – it is only available to KOLs. If we get positive response to the KOLs' postings, we launch the product for consumers, and the early buyers are also excited to talk about the product on social media."[44]

Further, KOLs can propose new product ideas based on their insights of their followers. Certain shades were proposed by KOLs and they could even have customized packaging for their fans. One such product, the Chinese Geography Eyeshadow Palette, was ranked #3 on TMall and was viewed over 180m times.[45]

Products were also co-created with KOLs. One such product was the Puppy Eyeshadow Palette, which was developed with Li Jiaqi, China's most famous beauty KOL and livestreaming salesperson. The shades in the palette were based on the colours of Li's dog, thus the "puppy" name. Li, known as the "King of Lipstick", with 44m followers on TikTok/Douyin and 4m followers on TMall, pre-sold 150,000 palettes before launch and 300,000 more in the first seconds of the official launch livestream in March 2020.[46]

Perfect Diary also did unexpected collaborations with China's *National Geographic* magazine, China Aerospace, the British Museum, New York's Metropolitan Museum of Art, and Discovery Channel. All put forward uniquely themed palettes that became collectibles and increased consumers' esteem of the brand due to the cultural connections.

This prolific innovation meant that Perfect Diary had an enormous number of SKUs – over 1,000 – much more than their competition. By contrast, the L'Oréal portfolio had only around 150 SKUs. This variety allowed Perfect Diary to satisfy very niche preferences of consumers in a way that other brands did not. Also, because the product was sourced from third-party suppliers, Perfect Diary could be nimble in getting products to market. Huang believed this was a key brand difference for Perfect Diary: "A large number of SKUs might not make sense for L'Oréal, but for us it is very meaningful because we use the AAARRR growth hacking framework (Awareness, Acquisition, Activation, Retention, Revenue, Referral). We worked with KOLs to satisfy the niche preferences of their fans with different SKUs as a pilot. Once it was proven to be a high-potential product, we extended to reach and acquire more customers. Even if 1% of our 60m customers prefer a particular colour or shade, it is a market of 600,000 customers. Even 0.1% of customers translates to 60,000 customers and we can serve them economically. And once the consumer knows that Perfect Diary will take care of my everyday needs including my niche preferences, consumer engagement level is very high."[47] By early 2021, Perfect Diary had over 50m followers across its various platforms and enjoyed an unheard-of e-commerce repurchase rate of 40%.[48]

Perfect Diary also engaged with consumers post-purchase and ultimately brought them on to their own direct sales channel, effectively converting public traffic (from other platforms) to private traffic (brand-controlled platforms) on social media. This is important as the costs of public traffic are steeply rising for brands in China, whereas the brand can better control the costs of private traffic, thus protecting their margins. How did Perfect

Diary do this? Once a purchase was made, the customer would be invited to join a Perfect Diary WeChat group chat. These were chat rooms of up to 500 individuals, hosted by a virtual AI-enabled beauty advisor who had a profile and appearance similar to the target consumer in order to make them feel more at ease and as if they were talking to a girlfriend. Xiaomeizi, as the beauty advisor is called, is a cute and charming way of saying "small beautiful one". There were two types of chat groups depending on where the consumers had been sourced. One type of consumers were those who had purchased through an online e-commerce or social commerce platform and joined through a promotional lucky money card containing a discount on the next purchase. The other type were consumers who had joined from offline pop-up stores or giveaways where they had scanned a QR code. The virtual beauty advisors communicated with consumers differently, using different tactics based on the source of recruitment and based on data-driven insights on how each group might be converted to purchase. Across both groups, AI beauty advisors shared tutorials on various products, answered any questions, and shared information on upcoming promotions and events. This had the impact of linking the consumers directly to the brand regardless of the original channel of purchase and meant that they could easily repurchase directly from the brand. It was observed that repurchase rates were even higher in these WeChat groups than on e-commerce.

Perfect Diary created a unique digital data platform, structured around the consumer with a single digital ID, which the Yatsen Group can use across all brands in the portfolio, making it an extremely powerful platform for growth. There's no multi-brand competitor that can say the same, as most customer insights and information live under individual brands. For example, consumers might be on Shu Uemura's database but this does not ladder up to a broader L'Oréal database that is accessible by other brands in the portfolio. In fact, the virtual beauty advisors on WeChat have the option to link users to Perfect Diary or one of the other Yatsen Group brands, depending on what might best suit the user's needs. Thus, Perfect Diary and Yatsen can as easily be thought of as owning a consumer segment, which they happen to sell a portfolio of colour cosmetics to, but the group could easily extend into other segments of interest to their consumer base.

In fact, in 2020, Yatsen Group purchased French skin care brand Galénic, European luxury skin care brand Even Lom, and Chinese derma-skin care brand Dr. Wu to do just this. Huang explains: "A single brand may fall in and out of favour, but a portfolio can probably stay on trend for a long time. Different brands follow different paths and it's hard to get every single step right. But at least we can build the infrastructure that benefits all. By infrastructure, I mean our supply chain, marketing machine, distribution channels and product experience. It's like we built the road for Perfect Diary. Other brands can run on the same road, but we don't just focus on the road ahead. We envision a highway and build it. Since we built a highway, we want more cars on it. Either we start new brands, or we buy existing ones. The latter is faster. Most of our supply chain, marketing, and IT processes can be directly adapted to new companies."[49] It has been estimated that with this DTC tech stack for e-commerce, marketing and consumer engagement, Yatsen Group could have any new brand – acquired or newly created – up and running and fully functional on e-commerce in a mere one to two days.[50]

To further drive sales through the private traffic channel, in 2019 the Yatsen Group started to open retail stores. The business had an ambitious plan to open 600 stores in two years, but rollout was slowed by the pandemic. By mid-2022, Perfect Diary was operating some 200 stores in China. The role of physical retail is two-fold: the first is to provide an immersive brand experience for consumers to play and experiment with products; the second is to convert offline shoppers into online private traffic owned by the brand. The business estimates that 65% of the store shoppers are new to the brand and thus represent private traffic conversion opportunities.[51] After purchasing products in stores, shoppers are given free gifts as incentives to enter the Perfect Diary WeChat groups. This winning market strategy has served as a guide to many other competing brands on how to regain control of their customers and convert them to private traffic.

In summary, Yatsen Group was created on the basis that two types of businesses could be fused – beauty and tech/social – and in the process create disruption and generate value. In leveraging behavioral, market, social and sales data, Perfect Diary has not only been able to stay ahead of trends better than its competitors, it has also been able to create and lead these trends. It has effectively changed product development from a more creative expression informed by R&D to a data-driven science with a pace and pulse that is more like a tech company. Perfect Diary takes products from concept to launch in less than six months, which is markedly faster than their global peers, who take 9–18 months to get a new product to market. And the results of this approach are abundantly clear: in just three years, Perfect Diary leapfrogged entrenched international rivals such as L'Oréal's

Maybelline and Estee Lauder's MAC brands to become China's #1 colour cosmetic brand. With more than 50 million followers on social media, it can now reach and sell to its audience directly with a near-zero marketing expense. This creates a growth fly-wheel that has a higher conversion from engagement to sales, and at a fraction of the typical industry cost. This social-enabled, data-driven beauty model saw astounding growth of 327% from 2018 to 2019, outpacing the top 10 market players, growing customers by 49% to 23m at the time of its IPO in 2019.[52]

In 2020, Yatsen Group decided it was time to take C-beauty and its fusion beauty-social business model global, launching Perfect Diary in Southeast Asia. Within a year, the brand had claimed top sales spots in multiple markets: #1 in lip sales in Malaysia, #1 in colour cosmetics in Singapore and Vietnam, and #1 in loose powder in the Philippines.[53] Back in China, despite the pandemic and contraction of planned retail store openings, sales were up 70.2% in the second half of 2020 (following lockdowns in Q1 and Q2); and as of end 2021, Yatsen Group was valued at US$12bn.[54]

UNSEATING GLOBAL MARKET LEADERS WITH SOCIAL INSIGHTS AND SOCIAL COMMERCE

Tang Binsen is the CEO and founder of Genki Forest Food Technology Company, China's fastest-growing beverage brand. However, Tang did not set out to be in the highly competitive yet historically low-margin soft drink and beverage business, duking it out with industry stalwarts such as The Coca Cola Company and PepsiCo. Yet, this former programmer and gaming executive spotted an opportunity for tech and data to shake up the consumer world after selling his first startup in mobile gaming for US$400m in 2014.

Tang noted that China already had enough strong players in e-commerce, gaming and social, but despite this level of development in digital platforms, there were still many lifestyle gaps in China compared to a country like the US. His feeling was that this was not attributable to a lack of technology, where in some cases China was ahead of the US, but rather to a lack of high-quality local brands. "China doesn't need any more good platforms," Tang wrote in an internal email in 2015, ostensibly referencing the mega-platforms of Baidu, Tencent and Alibaba. "But it does need good products."[55]

In turning his eye to brands and consumer products, Tang observed that of all the large and growing industries, fast-moving consumer goods (FMCG), particularly in food and beverage, were operating on a conventional model where tech and data had yet to be fully leveraged. Tang had no experience with FMCG or F&B, but this is very often the case with Chinese entrepreneurs. What he saw was an opportunity to disrupt consumer products with tech and data know-how. Tang set his sights on beverages with an aim to unseat global behemoths and local market leaders Coca Cola and PepsiCo in China.

To do so, Tang employed a data-driven strategy leveraging the consumer information and insights that could be gleaned from social media platforms. In fact, Genki Forest's operating model has more in common with a tech or media startup than with an FMCG company. Genki Forest started by populating an innovation product pipeline, defined by fringe trends starting to emerge on social media. This pipeline of products is teed up and ready to go, with beverages slated to be launched in quick succession, a pace typically only employed in the tech world, but here enabled by the availability of real-time consumer data on social media. In fact, the release of new products is informed by continuous data mining of sales and trends, enabling Genki Forest to bring new products to market at precisely the right moment that a trend is building and can be fully exploited. Factories are leased to ensure flexibility in manufacturing to enable the data-driven strategy, which requires quick pivots in production. And not surprisingly, Genki Forest has streamlined the route to market by going direct-to-consumer (DTC), with social commerce and e-commerce being the dominant channels of sales, skipping the distributor network and typical supermarket and convenience store retail channels. Social media and social commerce are both key marketing *and* selling channels to build the brand and drive consumer demand. A focus on heavily hyped online shopping festivals and high-profile digital influencers has helped to make Genki Forest the bestselling beverage brand in key selling periods, which has further boosted the profile and momentum of its now trend-setting beverage brands.

Since its inception, Genki Forest has rapidly scaled, selling its sugar-free sodas, milk teas and energy drinks in China and 40 other countries. Sales reached US$1.2bn in 2020 and the company valuation is US$6bn,[56] based on the highly valued potential of its unique data-driven business model. For comparison, Coca Cola's total revenue across all brands was US$37.5bn in 2020, which gave it a commanding 48% global market share. Genki Forest's valuation is the same size as the global annual sales of Coca

Cola Company's Sprite brand, one of the top ten soft drinks in the world by sales and sold in more than 190 countries.

FAST FASHION BECOMES REAL-TIME RETAILING

Unless you are a fashion-forward Gen Z female, you may not have heard of SHEIN (pronounced "she-in"), the online-only fast fashion company that has now eclipsed the ubiquitous Zara and H&M brands combined in terms of global sales. SHEIN is a business developed in China, but it is not intended for the China market. With shipping to 220 countries, SHEIN has its biggest market in the US, with other strong markets being the EU and Middle East.

In 2021, SHEIN's mobile app exceeded 7m active users a month in the US alone.[57] Google statistics show that users search for it three times more than Western brands like Zara. On TikTok, the hashtag #shein has captured over 6.2bn views. The momentum of this business is staggering: SHEIN has doubled its sales every year for eight years running. So why is SHEIN growing so fast and what makes them different from other fast-fashion brands, aside from their laser-focused Gen Z target and online-only model? Three key success factors of SHEIN are changing the game of fast fashion: speed, price and gamification, all enabled by social and social commerce.

The first factor of SHEIN's success is hyper-speed to market. Speed is, not surprisingly, a central tenet of fast fashion, and SHEIN is operating at a speed unmatched by any other player – and this speed is largely enabled by social media and social insights. For comparison, Zara pioneered fast fashion with inspired-by-the-runway looks in store within two to three weeks. Since the 1990s, this timing has been the gold standard in fast fashion and was pioneering at a time when most brands and department stores released new collections seasonally, two to three times a year. The core enabler of the Zara model is their uniquely flexible supply chain based on just-in-time manufacturing principles, a practice borrowed from Japanese automotive manufacturing and applied to textiles and clothing. For SHEIN, while speed is most certainly facilitated through their agile Chinese supply chain (which also relies on just-in-time manufacturing), supply chain is not the main lever of speed; data from social media is. Where SHEIN shines is in data-driven customer insights that enable the business to identity trends at hyper-speed and release of-the-moment styles within seven days of trending social media posts. That means if a Gen Z influencer sports a look on TikTok that starts trending, SHEIN has the look up for sale online within the week. With data-driven insights, SHEIN releases 2,000 SKUs a day, compared to Zara, which releases 1,000 new SKUs per month.[58]

These data-driven insights from social platforms are in fact the real engine of the business; they are a masterful combined effort of mining trending fashion and style posts on social media as well as their own social marketing activities to generate real-time data on their target audience and product portfolio. SHEIN uses a unique affiliate programme where up-and-coming influencers receive commissions for promoting the brand with posts of their outfits. Likes, shares, and comments yield real-time insights. SHEIN also partners with celebrity A-listers such as Katy Perry, Hailey Bieber, Lil Nas X and Yara Shahidi, which yields further insights on various segments and profiles within their customer base. SHEIN hosts live shows once a week on Instagram, and rather than having a single global Instagram or TikTok account, it maintains individual accounts by country to understand each market and customer more granularly. All this data becomes actionable insights for spotting trending fashions and styling in the market organically, rather than the fast-follower approach that other fast fashion brands employ, which relies on inspired-by-runway looks.

Another key lever in the fast-fashion industry, and for SHEIN, is price. Price has always been a fundamental promise of fast fashion: the runway look for less. For social media-loving Gen Z in particular, price is a highly sensitive factor with tipping point potential, as fashionable Gen Zers face the dilemma of having a relatively low disposable income but a high desire to have a fresh, of-the-moment look. SHEIN deeply understands this consumer due to their penetration in social media and is able to deliver the value this consumer expects in spades: where a summer dress at Zara or H&M averages around US$30, SHEIN delivers a similar dress for half that. In fact, given that the business was born in China, it might be surprising that SHEIN chooses not to compete in its home market. But a US$15 summer dress simply isn't a competitive price in China, which is why SHEIN seeks to dominate the overseas fast-fashion world, where it can deliver a price advantage. One of the social media trends SHEIN instigated was "shopping hauls". In this kind of social media post, a user buys a wide variety of products from SHEIN and tries them all on and models them for their followers. These kinds of posts have gone viral and are in fact now being leveraged by other DTC brands across product categories like fashion, skin care and cosmetics.

While much of the price advantage can be attributed to SHEIN's native understanding of manufacturing in China, which gives them a proximity-based advantage over other global fast-fashion brands also with production in China, the real source of their competitive advantage is knowing what to make and when, based on trending social content. This has evolved the just-in-time inventory management model pioneered in fashion by Zara to a real-time manufacturing model which is unsurpassed in efficiency.

Additionally, they have developed a unique manufacturing operations strategy by targeting underperforming, under-capacity factories with out-of-date inventory management systems. SHEIN does not buy these factories, but instead offers to partner with them and upgrade their operations with SHEIN's data-driven systems, powered by social media insights, in exchange for guaranteed demand for the factory. It's a win for both parties. SHEIN does not need to own the factories as assets but effectively controls them, guaranteeing their supply chain. The factory owners have fully utilized assets and learn how to manage a data-driven business based on real-time consumer preferences, thereby upskilling their operations.

Finally, using learnings from gaming and e-commerce, SHEIN also gamifies the shopping experience, making it extremely sticky and yet another source of data for insight and action. SHEIN's rewards system gives users points for activity and affiliate marketing. To gain points, users must check in daily or make product reviews, which demands daily active use on the app and on social media. Points are awarded for small tasks like email verification and for bigger tasks like engaging in special challenges, like posting videos of SHEIN shopping hauls. Points have monetary value, with 100 points equalling $1 that can be spent on SHEIN. Gamification drives engagement on their owned and social platforms, generating data, which in turn generates even more customer and product insights. It is a virtuous cycle of increasing engagement and brand omniscience. SHEIN has transformed fast fashion into real-time retail. Today it is valued at an eyewatering US$15bn, having eclipsed Zara in 2020.

BEING CLOSER TO THE CONSUMER ENABLES A MORE IMPACTFUL VALUE CHAIN FOR ALL PARTIES

Being closer to the consumer enhances the efficiency and effectiveness of the value chain for both businesses and their customers. Businesses gain deeper insights into their customers' preferences, needs and pain points. Socially created and informed brands can mine a treasure trove of data in the comments, likes, shares, and direct messages across platforms, which can be analyzed to understand their customers better. This understanding allows businesses to tailor their products and marketing strategies to meet customer demands more effectively. For decades, the goal of businesses and brands has been to get closer to their consumers. The future will see greater proximity than ever before, which businesses will need to harness to create more user-centric, personalized and relevant products, services and marketing.

This represents a win-win across both sides of the value chain and equation. As businesses use proximity and data to enable better customer understanding, build stronger brand-customer relationships, and become adaptable in an ever-evolving market, it also represents a benefit to customers. For customers, more customer-centric businesses mean products and services that are increasingly better able to meet their unique needs, sometimes even down to an individual level. Personalization enhances the overall customer experience and fosters stronger brand loyalty, enabling an upward spiral of value creation.

Chapter 4

Online Influencers – Going Virtual

All over the world, KOLs, or Key Opinion Leaders, are becoming the backbone of marketing for many brands and businesses. KOLs are people who are considered experts or thought leaders on topics ranging from fashion and cooking to health and wellness, or even in more serious spaces such as investing, business transformation and innovation. They can be celebrities, bloggers or simply people who have built a presence on social media. The commonality is that all have a strong personal brand and a significant following on social media platforms. Their followers look to them for recommendations and advice, and they can sway their followers' opinions and preferences – and thus their purchasing. Because of their ability to drive engagement on social media platforms, KOLs have the power to move markets, leveraging their enormous social media followings. Most likely if a product or trend has "gone viral", KOLs have had a hand in making that happen.

KOLs have large followings and when they share content related to a particular brand, it can reach a wider audience than the brand may be able to reach on its own. As a result of their power

65

and influence, some KOLs charge as much as millions of dollars for a single post on a single social media platform. For example, US media personality Kylie Jenner's starting price for Instagram is $1.2m a post, while her sister Kim Kardashian seems a relative bargain at a cool $1m. Singer-actress Selena Gomez, another popular KOL, charges $800,000 to $1m per post. And one of the most expensive KOLs is footballer Cristiano Ronaldo, who charges $1.6m per post on Instagram. These fees are outsize and enormous, but apparently so are the results. Cristiano Ronaldo's partnership with Nike reportedly resulted in a 300% increase in sales of the Nike Mercurial Vapor shoe, while Kylie Jenner's posts for Adidas reportedly resulted in a 10% increase in sales for the entire brand.

In China, where KOLs often host livestreaming sales on social commerce platforms, one famous influencer is Austin Li Jiaqi, known as the Lipstick King. Li sold US$1.7bn of cosmetics in 12 hours of livestreaming on Alibaba during China's 11/11 Singles Day sale, garnering 250m views.[59] Due to his ability to move markets, Li was listed in the 2021 TIME 100 list of Most Influential People. Another top KOL, Viya, sold US$1.25bn of products in her 14-hour livestream marathon in the same selling period.[60] KOLs in China not only charge fees, but sometimes also earn a percentage commission on sales, meaning they are potentially even more expensive than the seven-figure fees of top Hollywood celebrities and KOLs in the US.

While KOLs can be a powerful marketing tool, clearly the expense is large and increasing. This can give large brands pause and simply be cost-prohibitive for many small and medium-sized businesses. Further, there are concerns about the authenticity of KOLs' endorsements, particularly when they are paid eye-wateringly high sums for their post – consumers can feel that a KOL's endorsement is not genuine if it seems unlikely they would use the product or brand in real life. And when working with KOLs, brands relinquish a certain amount of control over their messaging and content. KOLs have their own voice and style, and a message has the potential to veer off track or ring false when using KOLs. Finally, KOLs are individuals, and they can be unpredictable – they are human after all. Brands run the risk of association with negative behaviours or messages from KOLs. Cancel culture is real globally, and if a KOL gets cancelled, it can impact brand reputation.

In China, for instance, quite a few celebrities have been cancelled by the government for various infractions, ranging from tax evasion to the more nebulous concerns of male influencers presenting as "too feminine". Chinese actor Deng Lun's social media accounts, with followers totalling 60m, were scrubbed by Chinese authorities in March 2022 when he was found guilty of tax evasion and fined RMB106m (US$16.7m).[61] International companies like Unilever and L'Oréal, as well as local companies like appliance maker Viomi and dairy company Junlebao, immediately dropped contracts with the Deng upon learning that he had hidden personal income earnings in fake business deals. The aforementioned KOL livestreamer Viya was also fined for tax evasion in 2021 to the tune of RMB1.34bn (US$210m).[62] These are just two examples among a slew of celebs who have been cancelled due to scandals, allegations of rape and even non-illegal behaviour deemed to not be in line with Chinese cultural norms.

VIRTUAL INFLUENCERS IN SOCIAL MEDIA AND SOCIAL COMMERCE

Cancel culture along with rising costs have pushed Chinese businesses to look for alternative solutions for consumer engagement on social media and social commerce. This has led to the invention and use of virtual KOLs – computer-generated influencers.

Imagine a computer-generated influencer who is highly aspirational, represents the ideal beauty and image standards, and whose persona can be curated by brands or marketing agencies. Thanks to advanced animation and AI, virtual influencers are nearly indistinguishable from humans, but unlike humans, they never age, gain weight, get embroiled in scandals, or say or do anything undesirable for a brand. Further to that, aside from the cost of creation, they do not have exorbitant fees or talent residual payments, they can work 24 hours a day, do not need breaks and can appear in many places at one time. These virtual idols always have perfect skin, a ready smile, a twinkle in the eye and are fast on their way to becoming a billion-dollar industry. Another big advantage is the ability of virtual KOLs to interact with and collect data from every single consumer – a data goldmine for brands and businesses.

It is not only the cost savings, data collection potential and flawless perfection of these virtual celebrities that appeal to both brands and consumers; it is also what it says about a brand that uses them, placing them in a forward-thinking, tech-savvy realm, even if they are simply selling something as basic as ice cream. And while it might seem that perfection is not all that relatable, Chinese consumers report this is part of a virtual idol's appeal. When a Shanghainese female consumer in her 30s was interviewed about the appeal of her favourite virtual influencer Ling, she reported that Ling's AI perfection made her "effortlessly cool" and a "moving art piece", and because Ling is so flawless, she does not compare herself to Ling in the same way she would to a real celebrity.[63] As a result, when engaging with Ling's content, she feels more inspired as she knows there are styles and looks she can try to emulate, but she's not disappointed, frustrated or left feeling inadequate if they do not quite work for her.

The incredible outcome for businesses is that the bottleneck of the content-hungry world of social media is no longer constrained by KOL or celeb casting, shooting, and editing. Now, highly curated custom content with compelling, aspirational virtual KOLs can be generated 24 hours a day. It is no surprise, then, that it was estimated in 2021 that the virtual influencer business in China was worth US$960m and is currently experiencing 70% year-on-year growth.[64]

GLOBAL BRANDS AND BUSINESSES ARE CATCHING ON

While the trend started in China, its success has led to a blossoming of virtual influencers being deployed by global brands in their marketing activities in the US and Europe. One of the most compelling examples is Lil Miquela. Lil Miquela is a virtual influencer created by Cain Intelligence and developed by Brud, a Los Angeles-based start-up. Brud is a software media company, started in 2014, that uses AI to create complex digital characters.

The Brud characters create social media profiles on platforms like Instagram and build large followings, thus attracting brands and sponsors. Voted "One of the 25 Most Influential People on the Internet" by *Time* in 2018, and with 3m followers on Instagram (as of February 2023),[65] Lil Miquela is one of Brud's most successful characters, who has attracted top global brands like Samsung, Prada and Calvin Klein.

Lil Miquela, also known as Miquela Sousa, is portrayed as a 19-year-old Brazilian-Spanish model and musician. One of the things that makes Lil Miquela unique is the level of detail in her design and creation. She has human facial features, expressions, body movements and poses that appear incredibly lifelike. Her creators have even gone to great lengths to create a backstory for her, including fake friends and family and even a boyfriend with whom she had a very public breakup in 2020. Her Instagram page is full of selfies showcasing her high-fashion street-wear style, her trendy music videos, and a faint whiff of woke Gen Z political activism. She loves travel, taco trucks and hanging with her hot-bot friends, often either dining out or making music together. Her music is on Soundcloud, Spotify and YouTube, and in real life she is represented by the famed Hollywood talent agency CAA. She has released a number of singles – her most popular, "Hate Me", has enjoyed 20 million streams on Spotify – and is reported to have a net worth of US$6m from her music and brand sponsorships.[66]

It's no surprise that Lil Miquela has been embraced by the fashion and brand world, with partnerships and collaborations with major global brands. One successful brand partnership was her collaboration with UGG, the US footwear company, in 2020. To promote their Classic Ultra Mini boots, UGG teamed up with Lil Miquela to create a series of Instagram posts and an online video campaign. The campaign featured Lil Miquela travelling, posing, and of course posting on Instagram wearing the boots in a variety of aspirational settings, from a snowy mountaintop to a fashionable urban street. While actual sales performance data is confidential, UGG stated that the campaign was an overwhelming success, with Lil Miquela's posts receiving tens of thousands of likes and a significant follow-on increase in brand engagement following the campaign.

What made the UGG and Lil Miquela partnership successful is no different from what makes real human talent and brand partnerships successful. There was clear alignment between Lil Miquela's followers – a group of young, fashion-forward and style-conscious women – and UGG's desired target audience. By tapping into this desirable audience, together Lil Miquela and UGG could generate a buzz around the product by leveraging Lil Miquela's unique persona and style to create visually appealing content that resonated with the audience. And because Lil Miquela's virtual influencer persona and fashion-forward style aligned perfectly with UGG's brand image, this made the partnership feel authentic and natural.

More recently, Lil Miquela collaborated with Calvin Klein and Prada, two iconic, historic fashion brands, both trying to reach out to younger audiences. For Calvin Klein, Lil Miquela collaborated on a campaign promoting their new fragrance, CK One. The campaign featured Lil Miquela in a series of Instagram posts and videos, wearing her styled take on Calvin Klein fashion and posing with the CK One fragrance bottle. The campaign used the hashtag #CKEveryone and was eminently successful at capturing the desired younger, more diverse audience. For Prada, the collaboration featured Lil Miquela in a series of Instagram posts and videos wearing Prada clothing and accessories – but again styled for a younger generation. The campaign, aimed at promoting Prada's use of innovative technology in their designs, used the hashtag #PradaRobot. Both campaigns were reported to have delivered unprecedented levels of engagement for the brands with younger audiences – a difficult feat for luxury brands who are better known for their classic, timeless styles and appeal to older, less trendy consumers.

While Lil Miquela is a virtual influencer, her impact on social media and popular culture is very real. She has become not only a symbol of the growing influence of virtual influencers and the potential they have to shape the future of social media and marketing, but also a revenue generator and money machine for her creators.

VIRTUAL INFLUENCERS ARE NOT WITHOUT CHALLENGES

Another fascinating virtual influencer use case demonstrates both the potential for business success as well as potential watch-outs for brands. When luxury fashion brand Balmain collaborated with the virtual influencer Shudu Gram on a campaign to promote their new collection, it was initially regarded as successful for the brand and a progressive move at being more inclusive in luxury fashion. Shudu Gram is a virtual South African supermodel, fashion queen and influencer in her 20s created by Cameron-James Wilson, a British fashion photographer who taught himself 3D modelling from watching videos on YouTube.

Shudu Gram was one of three models who appeared in a campaign called "Balmain's Army of Virtual Models". With a goal of showcasing diversity and promoting inclusivity, Balmain employed Black, Asian, and European virtual talent to promote their latest collection. The campaign used advanced 3D modelling techniques to create highly realistic images of the models, making the three ethnically diverse models largely indistinguishable from real-life talent. These images and videos were shared widely on Instagram and other social media platforms, quickly going viral, largely because of the unbelievable realism of the virtual models. The campaign generated significant buzz on social media, garnered millions of views, and was regarded as highly successful in promoting Balmain's latest collection.

Yet, while many praised Balmain for its forward thinking in both technology as well as social diversity and inclusivity, the campaign also drew some criticism. Some argued that the use of virtual models perpetuated unrealistic beauty standards and that the creation of the models could be seen as a form of cultural appropriation. Shudu Gram as black model drew more criticism than the other virtual models, potentially because her creator was a white male. Some critics said it was black beauty as viewed through a white lens, others called it a form of racism, and still others called it virtual slavery as a black "person" was generating income for a white male owner.

This particular controversy shed light on an important topic that creators and marketers will need to wrestle with: Is it potentially exploitative or insensitive – or even cultural appropriation – to create virtual influencers of specific racial and ethnic profiles?

So while virtual influencers are showing lots of promise, the Balmain case demonstrates some potential risks in this nascent phase. Other risks, controversies and questions exist as well. For example, will virtual influencers connect as deeply and as authentically with their followers? Many people argue that virtual influencers are not "real" people and therefore lack the relatability of human influencers. While we can see that engagement with virtual influencers has been high, is this early engagement driven by novelty which will eventually wear off?

Also, do the brands that use them employ responsible marketing? Do virtual influencers perpetuate unreasonable physical and beauty standards at a time when society and consumers are trying to break free from these previously held beliefs? And is there the potential for deception with virtual influencers? It has been observed that in many cases it is not immediately clear to audiences that these characters are not real people. Some consumers and social media users have even reported feeling deceived and misled, and requested that virtual influencers be flagged as "not real" to avoid confusion.

And as an emerging area in advertising, should there be regulation for virtual spokespeople? Today, unlike human influencers, virtual influencers do not have to adhere to the same guidelines and regulations around advertising and endorsements, making it more difficult for audiences to understand when they are being marketed to, and thus representing potential issues in transparency and disclosure.

So while virtual influencers have gained popularity in recent years, there are still many questions and concerns surrounding their use. As the industry continues to evolve, it will be important for brands and marketers to consider these issues and work to address them in order to maintain the trust and credibility of their audiences.

WHY VIRTUAL INFLUENCERS WILL LIKELY GROW AND THRIVE

Virtual influencers do still bring a great many advantages to brands and businesses who need to break through in the increasingly cluttered environments of social media and social commerce. These advantages will likely continue to attract and fascinate both consumers and marketers. For one, virtual KOLs can be created to have outstanding qualities that make them stand out from real-life influencers. For example, Lil Miquela's unique persona makes her consistently more interesting, memorable and engaging than most real-life influencers.

Virtual influencers can generate unlimited creative possibilities as they are not limited by the physical constraints of the real world and can be placed in any setting and wear any outfit without the need for expensive location shoots, stylists, or wardrobe changes. Quite literally, virtual influencers could be sent to the moon! Yet they also provide great consistency and quality of appearance. Virtual influencers do not change or age, which makes them recognizable and memorable to their followers and makes them durable assets for brands. They never get caught out in a tracksuit and bed head walking their dog. Compare this to real-life influencers, who may change their appearance suddenly, have a bad hair or skin day, or even have plastic surgery – these changes could be confusing and alienating to their followers, and potentially render them out of character for the brands they represent.

There are endless opportunities for collaboration with virtual KOLs. They never have scheduling conflicts, can appear 24 hours a day, can be in multiple locations simultaneously, and can work with any brand or category of products regardless of geographic location. This makes it easier for brands to work with virtual influencers, removing some of the very real constraints in working with human influencers. But perhaps the most persuasive argument is the ultimate control that creators and brands have in working with virtual influencers. Messaging and content can be carefully calibrated to fit the brand's objectives whereas human influencers may have personal opinions or beliefs in conflict with the brand's messaging.

It is undeniable that virtual influencers offer a unique and innovative approach to modern marketing, and as technology continues to advance and become more sophisticated, it is likely we will see their use become ever more prevalent and mainstream. What will be a space to watch is the intersection and integration of virtual influencers with AI. We can expect that AI will enable virtual influencers to interact with audiences in more personalized and dynamic ways as they learn about consumers' preferences and behaviours.

Chapter 5

The Future of Shopping – Powered by Social, AI and Big Data

In recent years, the model of retail has significantly evolved. Beyond the segment of social commerce described earlier, how consumers access and purchase goods and services has most certainly been transformed by digital platforms and e-commerce. However, bricks-and-mortar versus online e-commerce is now an outdated and simplistic way to think about the variety of ways that consumers can access information, interact with products, experience products, and ultimately purchase. To understand where the future of consumer buying is headed, let us look at the evolution of consumer purchasing globally in recent years.

The traditional retail model, where consumers physically visit a store to make purchases, was the norm for over a hundred years. Despite the barcode scanning technology that came along in the 1980s, this model had limited visibility into consumer behaviour and shopping patterns. There was a significant time lag in the data that was available as it was captured on a monthly basis and issued yet another month after that. Further, unless someone was part of a loyalty programme and then scanned a card at the time of purchase, it was also difficult to tie the purchase to individual consumers or households for demographic insights. As a result, the ability to optimize operations and promotions was limited. When e-commerce entered the picture, yet more visibility was possible as purchasing data was real-time and also directly tied to names and addresses, enabling a more granular understanding of how, when and why individual consumers and households purchased.

Then the O2O, or Online-to-Offline, model was retailers' blended answer to a more seamless shopping experience for consumers, where customers could browse and purchase products online but with an integration of the physical store, either to experience products firsthand prior to purchase or for pick-up in store. In this way, retailers were able to leverage both their physical presence and the convenience of online shopping to better serve their customers. However, as technology evolved and smartphones became nearly ubiquitous, new channels of commerce opened up to retailers.

The omnichannel model leveraged the mobile component to take the O2O model a step further by offering a seamless shopping experience across multiple channels, including online, in-store and mobile. In this model, customers can more discretely optimize and personalize along their shopping journey. For example, customers have access to multiple channels for information, experiences and purchase – typically a website (either retailer-run or e-commerce platform), a mobile app, and physical stores. Customers can browse products, try them, check inventory, make purchases, and receive sales support – all in a way that meets their unique, individual preferences. Retailers and brands can serve them tailored, and therefore more relevant, promotions and offers based on their shopping histories, location, or other preferences. Additionally, unified inventory systems enable both retailers and customers to check the availability of products across channels, ensuring products are available when and where customers want them. Flexible fulfilment delivers greater convenience in that customers have multiple options for receiving products, including home delivery, in-store pickup, and curbside pickup. For the retailer, these features typically deliver a lower cost of conversion for the sale for a more efficient marketing spend. Further, omnichannel also provides the retailer the opportunity to control the brand not only in the consistency of presentation and expression, but also in the shopping experience, which has the effect of driving trust and loyalty with consumers. The omnichannel shopping experience leveraging technology and data has provided consumers with a seamless, efficient shopping experience that is both personalized, convenient, and better meets their needs and preferences, and as a result is the gold standard of marketing and retailing in most of the world.

However, with the increasing prevalence of AI, data from social, and social commerce, retail today has an opportunity to further evolve the experience. And in fact, China has already done so and provides a valuable model for the rest of the world to emulate. In 2016, Jack Ma, founder of the Alibaba Group and the pioneer of e-commerce in China, coined the phrase "New Retail" in his annual letter to company shareholders. Ma envisioned a new generation of retail that would eclipse all other models. He explained: "Pure e-commerce will be reduced to a traditional business and replaced by the concept of New Retail – the integration of online, offline, logistics, and data across a single value chain."[67]

This grand vision for the future of retail painted a picture of a fully integrated universe of offline and online retail as well as logistics, enabled by data analytics and AI to create a seamless and frictionless world for consumers to access goods and services. New Retail represents an entirely new value constellation for consumers and retailers, both of whom will ultimately benefit in the digital and technology retail revolution.

While this may sound like a Chinese version of omnichannel retailing, the way New Retail sets itself apart is the innovation around customer experience and delivery as well as the scale and speed of service and implementation which leverages new and emerging technologies as enablers to transform the industry. Further, New Retail acknowledges that consumers experience the retail world holistically and that "offline" and "online" are business constructs rather than helpful frames for consumers. Today consumers interact with brands and engage and experience their products and service across a variety of channels, typically purchasing in the channel that is most convenient for them. Consumers do not mentally delineate the places or occasions of brand interaction or purchase, and the expectation is that wherever they seek to experience a product or brand, it is there in a frictionless, seamless fashion for them. Brands that ask for even a small additional effort to purchase are often forgone for another brand that makes it easier to experience and purchase.

New Retail asserts that traditional retail brands must integrate online brand experience and purchase, while digital-native verticals should conversely consider physical experiences and purchasing for their customers. To realize the potential and ambition of New Retail means to recognize how consumers today live and to respond with digitally enabled customer journeys that deliver unique, memorable and frictionless experiences.

"NEW RETAIL" AS A MODEL FOR THE FUTURE OF SUPERMARKET SHOPPING

Jack Ma sought to achieve his New Retail vision with Alibaba Group's new supermarket experience called Hema, which launched in 2016. Hema, known in English as Fresh Hippo, was created as a lab for Alibaba Group to experiment with new approaches and technologies that would ultimately shape and define New Retail.

At the time, grocery seemed an unusual choice for a New Retail experiment. The model was fraught with challenges, such as managing cold storage logistics while maintaining profitability – products needed different temperatures and many fragile or oddly shaped items were not stackable. Additionally, there was a dilemma in the industry on whether to use physical stores as order fulfilment centres versus regional warehouses for distribution. Using retail stores as distribution hubs was expensive as it relied on order fulfilment to be managed by individuals in local stores. Further, product availability could not be guaranteed as physical stores sometimes faced stock-outs from foot-traffic shoppers. On the other hand, regional warehouses represented an incremental set of cost structures around inventory and logistics – large expenses in an industry where margins are notoriously slim.

Facing these very same challenges, overseas large players struggled to crack the integration of offline to online in grocery. Marks & Spencer in the UK acquired a 50% stake in online grocery retailer Ocado with a view to expand its online capabilities, while Amazon in the US acquired premium grocery retailer Whole Foods to achieve a physical retail presence.[68] It was precisely for this reason that Alibaba Group sought to explore New Retail in the context of grocery – imagining if the challenging problem of digitalizing grocery could be cracked, that the vision for New Retail could be realized in other contexts.

The China grocery market, though, was quite different from the US or Europe. A whopping 73% of shoppers bought fresh foods like meat, eggs and produce at neighbourhood wet markets, whereas only 22% bought through supermarkets and 3% through e-commerce.[69] Because consumers desired the freshest food possible, their habit was to purchase daily – either early in the morning or on the way home from work – feeling that wet markets provided the freshest foods because they were restocked daily, straight from countryside farms. Supermarkets were viewed as places to buy packaged foods off the shelf, whereas e-commerce was typically used to buy heavy or bulky products such as laundry detergent, drinks or toilet paper and have these delivered straight to their door. However, given the rising middle class and increasing disposable income in China, particularly in mega-cities such as Shanghai, Beijing and Guangzhou, Alibaba Group saw an opportunity to upgrade the consumption and grocery habits of middle-class, urban working consumers, who would be open to a more convenience-driven offer.

The first Hema store opened in Shanghai's Pudong district in January 2016 with little fanfare. This first store was seen as a laboratory in which Alibaba Group could quietly experiment with the New Retail concept. Six months later, with the model proven, Hema began to roll out more stores across China. The Hema model featured innovative, signature concepts like a live seafood market with an integrated restaurant where the seafood could be selected by the customer, prepared by chefs, and directly eaten on site. Waiters and sometimes robots delivered the dishes to customers who, impressed with the quality, often then purchased more seafood to take home. This space featured large and exotic seafood such as 5 kg (11 lb) Alaskan King Crabs, which attracted many photographs and videos, becoming a viral phenomenon on Chinese social media. As seafood is expensive in China and represents wealth and prestige, the integrated fresh seafood restaurant experience even became a draw for domestic tourists travelling to Shanghai or Beijing for holidays. Independent social media blogs and vlogs offered Hema travel and shopping tips for visitors.

Brightly coloured and lush fresh produce were displayed near the entrance to attract consumers. All fresh produce featured Hema's Full Traceability Program. Consumers could scan a QR code to trace the source of the products and determine, to the exact minute, when they left the farm. Other information available included the temperature of transport, the route, suppliers' official government certifications and even suggested recipes and customer reviews. Hema launched a private-label brand for produce that had colour-coded packaging corresponding to the day of the week, so consumers would know that this was today's product, and that yesterday's products had been removed.

Stores themselves had few service staff (apart from the restaurant) as they were almost completely digitalized, with product information and pricing on barcode shelf tags and a completely cashless checkout process enabled by digital payments. Most staff on the floor were those fulfilling the online orders for which the local store served as a distribution centre.

When ordering online, orders of fresh produce were guaranteed to arrive within 30 minutes, with no minimum order – the only restriction was that the order be within a 3 km radius of the store. This model not only represented unmatched convenience for customers, who had only experienced 3–4-hour delivery windows for other fresh goods suppliers, but it was also a cost-saver for Hema as it meant that fresh products could be delivered using only insulated boxes and bags, with no need for a cold storage supply chain. Hema even introduced a night service of health and medicine products with the same guaranteed 30-minute delivery in Shanghai and Beijing.

To meet the 30-minute delivery times, orders were prepared in store within a maximum limit of 10 minutes. Thanks to the digitalization of inventory, the digital purchasing channel (whether app or web) only presented real-time available products to the shopper, so stock-outs or gaps in fulfilment were deftly avoided. Baskets on an overhead conveyor belt system moved through the store with a computer navigating the basket's quickest route to complete the order. To ensure quick retrieval of goods, order-picking staff were specialized in one area of the store and equipped with a terminal with a digital read-out of the order so that they were ready and waiting when the basket reached the docking station to place the goods inside. Not only was this efficient but it also represented another form of in-store experience and engagement for the shoppers in the physical store as they watched online orders being adroitly fulfilled.

Within 18 months, 13 stores in 3 cities were opened that enjoyed 3-5 times sales per unit area versus other area supermarkets; Hema reported an unheard-of 35% conversion rate on the app; and 60% of all orders were from online channels.[70] Customers made 4.5 purchases per month on average, shopping 50 times a year.[71] All interactions with customers were captured in data which enabled Hema's AI engine to make product recommendations, advise on relevant promotions, and improve delivery service on an individual customer level. Internally, data helped ensure that at every store, the products most sought after locally were always fresh and available, and helped the store manage inventory more carefully, such that there was no spoilage or wastage.

Hema additionally built strong relationships with suppliers, promising no slotting fees, ever.[72] They also formed partnerships with provincial government agriculture departments to help them develop methods for higher and more profitable outputs for the farmers, facilitating economic development in rural areas.

This behaviour was disruptive in an industry where high slotting fees were the norm and back-door deals were often a necessity for suppliers to secure distribution. These partnerships enabled Hema to build strong private-label brands, comprising 10% of its sales, a remarkable shift in a market where private label was not popular (as consumers preferred branded products for quality assurance) and in other retailers only comprised 3–5% of sales.[73]

While the planned expansion slowed in 2020 and 2021 due to the pandemic, by 2022 Hema boasted some 350 stores in 27 cities across China, targeting concentrated urban centres with populations of over 1 million.[74] Hema's data-driven model, supply chain management and supplier partnerships formed a powerful value constellation which enabled higher margins compared to typical grocery businesses. Hema operated with higher sales per square metre and less wastage, and delivered better consumer convenience, creating a sticky shopping experience that generated consumer loyalty. As of January 2022, Hema's high-tech grocery model was valued at US$10bn.[75]

BIG DATA AND AI ENABLE A NEW CUSTOMER EXPERIENCE: AUTONOMOUS DELIVERY

In the US and some of Europe, with an annual membership fee of US$119 (as of August 2021), Amazon Prime members can receive delivery of eligible goods overnight. When Prime launched in 2014, this was a massive leap forward in challenging conventional retail, which accelerated the fundamental shift to online in consumer buying habits in the US and Europe. Since then, the delivery window for some goods has shortened even further, to a matter of hours, with the offer of same-day delivery. However, compare this to China and it is wildly disappointing from a consumer point of view. This is because consumers in China measure delivery not in hours, but minutes.

It is possible, for example, to order from e-commerce or a food-delivery site or app and enjoy a wide variety of goods delivered within 30 minutes, on average. This could be anything from a basket of groceries to a flat-panel television to a pair of sneakers – even a single cup of coffee can be delivered. No order is too small in monetary value or too large in physical size for instant delivery. Thus, it is not surprising that in the increasingly frictionless shopping universe of Chinese consumers, delivery time has become an important variable in consumer choice. Between multiple apps and order possibilities, the fastest delivery wins the purchase.

This consumer expectation and industry promises have had the unintended effect of creating driver safety issues. As companies attempt to minimize delivery times with timing algorithms and incentive schemes for drivers, drivers sometimes put themselves in harm's way, risking injury and even death. With both public and government pressure to reform delivery practices, alongside customer pressure to shorten delivery times, companies started to pilot autonomous vehicle delivery in 2016 in a race to shorten the standard delivery time for goods, and to do so safely.

Cut to 2020, where in a pandemic, autonomous delivery proved to be an ideal solution, given the need for contactless delivery. The rollout of autonomous delivery was thus given a shot in the arm. Self-driving vehicles were widely deployed, for example in Wuhan for contactless delivery of medical supplies to Wuhan Ninth Hospital, COVID-19 ground zero in China. Autonomous delivery was scaled further by e-commerce company JD.com in 2021, with self-driving fleets serving 200 cities with a "delivery-in-minutes" service. During the popular "618" shopping festival the same year, JD.com recorded delivering a skin care set by autonomous delivery[76] to a customer in Changshu city just 4 minutes after the customer paid the remaining balance of her pre-sale order.

As Alibaba's Chief Technology Officer Cheng Li says, "Autonomous driving technology is becoming a core technology in the digital era."[77] Autonomous delivery, which still looks like the stuff of science fiction in most other countries, is now table stakes in the e-commerce game in China. And while the autonomous vehicle delivery innovation is remarkable in and of itself, what makes this technology more than a novelty – and fuels it as a highly commercial application – is data. While autonomous vehicles do deliver more safely without the need for human operators, effectively addressing safety concerns, they are not the only key to unlocking shorter delivery times. They do not drive faster, nor are they immune to traffic. Faster delivery times are powered by data-driven systems of smart distribution hubs with hyper-local orientation, with goods pre-stocked in anticipation of future orders. Real-time data continuously updates to ensure local distribution hubs have the right type and amount of stock based on time-of-day shopping patterns, neighbourhood demographics, and types of goods commonly needed. This looks very different from one neighbourhood to the next. Imagine a family in the suburbs being able to get diapers delivered in mere minutes versus a young urbanite wanting a trending cosmetic product to change up their look for a night out. Inventory is calibrated with real-time data multiple times a day, resulting in an entirely next-level realization of "just in time" inventory management that enables agility in order fulfilment.

So while driver safety and the pandemic's contactless delivery needs no doubt propelled autonomous delivery to scale, data was the key that unlocked the commercial impact of this innovation in creating tangible value through increasingly frictionless shopping in the form of shorter delivery times for customers.

AI AND DATA-HUNGRY "NEW RETAIL" MAKES FAST FOOD SMART

New Retail is data-hungry, but with AI now being layered on top, data becomes smart, self-learning, and always improving. Yum! China gives a window into the future of quick service restaurants (QSR) – a truly seamless and frictionless browsing and buying experience, powered by data and AI, that is fully flexible, adaptable, and customizable by the consumer or shopper. Interestingly, QSR is not a typically tech-heavy sector globally as the traditional business model is reliant on convenient locations, food quality, and consistently high levels of cut-through advertising as key levers of the business. However, in China, data and AI as enablers are fundamentally changing the way the game is played, and Yum! China is leading the way.

Yum! China, the operator of the Taco Bell, KFC and Pizza Hut franchises, is China's biggest fast-food operation. In fact, Yum!

Brands is an American-originated company, but in 2016 Yum! China spun off and became locally owned and operated. Since this time, Yum! China has invested in building a digital ecosystem, harvesting data and leveraging technology, and has emerged as an innovative leader in New Retail and data-driven business in China.

The engine of the business is its digital ecosystem of the KFC and Pizza Hut super apps and the 240 million Chinese consumers who use them (as of end-2019). The apps provide an immersive experience with social aspects that make them sticky and allow the brands to engage with consumers wherever they are on a broad range of topics – not only food, but also music, sports, gaming and entertainment. Within each app are personalized digital features such as coupons and vouchers, privilege memberships, e-commerce, payment options, and corporate social responsibility activities. The data enables a wealth of insights at customer, city, and store level, which helps to drive highly differentiated and more effective store formats, locations and menu items. As digital marketing accounts for 60% of Yum!'s marketing spend, real-time data powers a flexible yet targeted approach based on consumer preferences. Yum! can effectively nudge and guide marketing programmes in real time to build awareness and loyalty faster than ever before. With data as a core enabler, Yum! is able to more effectively manoeuvre the key levers in the fast-food business model.

In 2019, Yum! went one step further on its innovation-with-data journey in the form of AI-enabled menus and recommendations for each diner, with personalized customer interaction and trade-up opportunities based on local tastes. The AI-powered menu has already boosted average per-order spending by 1% – equivalent to US$840m worth of fried chicken and pan pizzas each year.[78]

But data and AI are not just about marketing and upselling. They help Yum! China forecast demand, cut food waste, deliver menu innovation, optimize supply chain management, and create delivery and in-store operational efficiencies. For delivery, AI schedules the cooking and preparation time of orders that include both food and beverages, so that the food arrives warm and the beverages cold. An AI-driven dispatching system and logistics overflow support makes the relationship between customers, riders, and stores even more frictionless.

Back-of-house operations use AI-based technology to improve sales forecasting, which leads to better inventory management and store labour scheduling. Tailor-made algorithms identify changing data patterns at the store level, such as location, sales performance, weather, promotions, and holidays, to enable the quick reallocation of resources to new roles and growth areas. The company is also rolling out smart watches that enable managers to closely monitor the ordering and serving status of restaurants to quickly identify and rectify any issues before they become service bottlenecks.

In store, technology makes for an immersive customer experience. Ice cream is served by robotic arms. Customers can control the background music through their mobile phones.[79] Many stores have no cashiers to take orders or process payment – in fact, you would be hard-pressed to find human beings other than customers in the front of the restaurants. Orders are made on an interactive screen with a chatbot and are completely cashless, taking only digital payments made by AI-powered facial recognition software. Today, between delivery and in-store, more than 60% of orders are made digitally.[80]

Ultimately for Yum! China, technology and AI bring precision and personalization to every interaction with the KFC and Pizza Hut brands. Based on its innovative tech-powered approach to transforming food and food service, in 2020 Yum! China was named to *Fast Company* magazine's annual list of the World's Most Innovative Companies and was named as one of China's 10 most innovative companies. Not many restaurants end up on either list, which is typically dominated by the usual suspects of technology, pharmaceuticals and startup disruptors.

Since its spin-off from its American parent company in 2016, Yum! China has experienced significant growth. In the year ending 31 March 2021, its net income increased by more than 72% over the previous year,[81] and its stock price on the NYSE rose from $28.14 in November 2016 to $61.44 in August 2021.[82]

LEVERAGING SOCIAL MEDIA, DIGITAL AND AI FOR A NEW CUSTOMER JOURNEY

Armed with real-time data, real-time responsiveness, and AI predictive technologies that enable a deeply consumer-centric approach, any business has the opportunity to disrupt its industry. To imagine a new future for its consumers and operations, a business only needs to imagine what a more seamless, frictionless and personalized customer journey might look like. Also, when businesses have real-time insights, they can unlock a new level of sensitivity to consumers and deliver real-time responsiveness, effectively anticipating consumer needs at every step. When a business moves from answering consumer needs to anticipating them, it undoubtedly soars past the competition, potentially even creating a new standard for the industry.

While New Retail is a concept that can be directly leveraged, what we can observe is that it all starts with the concept of convergence of digital and retail, which is enabled by data (largely from social), and is much wider and deeper than the concept of omnichannel in play in the US and Europe. As in the Yum! China example, New Retail merges physical, digital, data and technology to make the business smart and self-learning, which drives a virtuous cycle of continuous improvement.

In fact, in China, many Western brands are already effectively delivering the New Retail experience because they must compete and defend against local brands. Brands ranging from Nike to Zara to Louis Vuitton are delivering game-changing retail experiences, driving brand preference with consumers. For example, at Zara, according to a local store manager in Shanghai, 70% of purchases happen on a mobile phone in the fitting room. When asked why in the fitting rooms instead of at the cashier counter, the main answer is that consumers find it more convenient to try on and scan the tag of the item in the fitting room and have it delivered to home – then they don't have to carry a shopping bag around. Further, if their ideal size or colour is not available in that particular store, they can still get exactly what they want, delivered straight to their door, usually by the next day. Zara's app also offers promotions where buying coupons are unlocked real-time with the posting of fitting room selfies.

What is curious is that these social, digital and AI insights have yet to travel back to these international companies' home markets to change the game at home. That said, IKEA has launched its store of the future in Shanghai, a pilot programme to explore New Retail possibilities for the business that could be exported globally if proven in China. Retail indeed represents one of the major areas where businesses can look to Asia, and particularly China, for the future of how brands are exploring the future of consumer experience.

Chapter 6

Digital Platforms: Assembling Ecosystems of Value

When we look at some of the most valuable social and digital platforms in the world and their goals with regard to use cases and growth, a pattern emerges. The pattern is about capturing *more* – more time of users, higher levels of engagement and interaction, and ultimately larger amounts of their users' spend. The businesses that have succeeded in building powerful global social platforms have done this through organic growth of their own platforms as well as acquisition of new platforms to create ecosystems of value that seek to cross-pollinate users – think Meta with Facebook and their acquired Instagram and WhatsApp platforms.

What is most notable about these ecosystems is that, more often than not, they are the cobbling together of existing businesses or offers to broaden and explode the overall system's utility and reach. Ultimately this yields growth via a richer ecosystem of value, rather than growth facilitated by a new-to-the-world technology or invention. In fact, when incremental innovation better meets consumers' needs, it can be significantly more powerful than a new-to-the-world invention. And when users' needs are better served with incremental innovation, the business can be more easily and rapidly scaled, largely because there's no learning curve – the platform often builds on existing user behaviour. Instead, intuitive, value-add functionality is bolted on to well-understood platforms, and massive social and economic impact is generated in the process. Perhaps the best example of this is the world's most valuable and powerful digital ecosystem: Tencent's WeChat, China's pervasive social, e-commerce, messaging, payments and booking app. It's no wonder that Elon Musk announced his wish to transform Twitter into a similar "everything app" that emulates WeChat's powerful digital ecosystem.[83]

THE MOST VALUABLE DIGITAL ECOSYSTEM IN THE WORLD

By all reports and analysis, there is no one component of WeChat that demonstrates unassailable technological superiority or invention. What is unique to it is its assembly of features and functionality based on a vision of a broad digital ecosystem that can serve its users across many aspects of daily life.

WeChat, or Weixin as it is known in China, has evolved from its start in 2011 as an instant messaging app to become the "operating system" of China, meeting the daily needs of over 1.27bn monthly active users[84] across China and, more broadly, Asia. This makes WeChat one of the most successful software products in history; it has catapulted its parent company Tencent into one of the top 10 companies in the world by market capitalization[85] alongside tech giants such as Apple, Microsoft and global behemoths like Saudi Aramco and Visa.

How did an instant messaging app become arguably the world's most powerful digital ecosystem of services? Over 10 years, WeChat consistently innovated to add more features, functionality and cross-pollination with other companies' apps and services, such that it has become a portal to all features of daily life. On WeChat, you can instant message, search the internet, share photos or documents, send or receive payment with vendors or individuals, book a taxi or rideshare car service, book a flight, train or hotel, manage the payment of your utilities and mobile phone, apply for a loan or manage your wealth portfolio, donate to charity, access your medical records, shop any of your favourite brands, book gym classes and manage your membership, stream videos, order food delivery, buy tickets for movies, concerts and sports games, conduct group buys, sell or buy used goods, find housing to buy or rent... the list is virtually endless. A whole book could be written about WeChat and its functionality, but more important than what WeChat enables users to do is how it architected such a meaningful value constellation for users that life without WeChat is unimaginable to those who use it. The app is so transformative that when many Chinese travel to countries where WeChat is less penetrated, they say they feel as if they have stepped 10 years back in time.

Initially, in 2011, with WeChat offering only the free text messaging function, the three big mobile phone operators joined up to collectively oppose the app and lodged complaints with government oversight agencies, seeing WeChat as a free SMS service and therefore a threat to their existing large revenues from SMS services. To convert mobile providers into allies, WeChat partnered with China Unicom (one of the big three), developing a data card pilot programme to demonstrate how mobile providers could make even more revenue from data charges than SMS fees – thus demonstrating the power of the ecosystem beyond Tencent.

In the first stage of development, frequent releases surprised users with new functionality such as group chat and voice messaging. However, WeChat was not growing rapidly as there were several local competitors – for example the dominant internet chat provider QQ had recently launched a mobile version. It was with voice messaging that the app really took off, as voice messaging was new and different and represented real communication with intonation and emotion for users – something that people were eager to try. Mobile phones did not have voicemail functionality and answering machines were not the norm in China, where many homes did not have land lines and had already leapfrogged to mobile. Voice and video calling soon followed. A distinct difference between WeChat and other messaging or social apps is that there is no way to see when or if a message has been read. This is because WeChat's creator and chief developer Allen Zhang felt that "social interaction should have a threshold … When you know I have received your message, it pressures me to respond."[86]

Another breakthrough innovation was Moments, a social feed where users could post photos and videos visible to those in their contact list – this further differentiated it from other chat-only providers and even had functionality that differentiated it from social apps which were based on text posts with photos being rarely posted. Also, unlike other social media, pictures, likes or comments could not be seen by friends of friends, so there was more of a feeling of a closed social group with privacy, with WeChat seeking to "create a tool that belonged to the mobile network from the inside out".[87] Later, a new and unique function, People Nearby, enabled users to find people and make new friends by shaking their phone, which would signal to users who also had People Nearby open and who were within a certain radius that they were open to connect and chat. This first stage of development created a useful communication and social platform that amassed 100 million users in 433 days.[88]

In the second stage of development, digital payments and a Services section of the app were added. A bank account could be linked to the profile and through the new WeChat Pay offer, users could send payments to a variety of institutions as well as individuals. The new Services functionality allowed WeChat to actively bring in third-parties such as ride-hailing apps, utility companies and travel websites as partners. Buttons were added which allowed users to tap to access their utility bills to view and pay them. All hardcopy bills sent by mail featured a QR code that could be scanned to pay and prompted users upon doing so to link to their WeChat for future convenience. There were buttons to book travel via third-party providers that consumers were already familiar with, with special pricing for WeChat users. Users could tap a transportation button to order a taxi or hail a ride-sharing car, also using existing providers. In restaurants and shops, users could scan QR codes to pay conveniently, without the need for cash exchange. Money could be sent to friends and contacts in the chat function of the app, enabling easy bill sharing. However, as digital payments were still nascent, WeChat decided to implement a novel play to give users a reason to send money digitally with a "hongbao" feature. This was a playful digital take on the practice of giving hongbao, or red envelopes with cash gifts – a practice that is customary over Chinese New Year as well as a way of saying thank you in Chinese culture. As intended, this kickstarted the use of WeChat Pay and helped it rapidly close the gap with competitor Alipay, who had launched more than a year earlier.

By integrating payment to many providers through the Services section of the app, WeChat started becoming a convenience hub for users, serving as a booking, planning and payment portal for frictionless living. The market-leading ride-hailing app DiDi (the Uber of China) operates within WeChat, and the majority of DiDi users access the service through WeChat rather than DiDi's own app. China Telecom reported that most monthly mobile bills and pay-as-you-go SIM top-ups were paid within WeChat and not through their own payment channels. Initially WeChat had a plan to charge third-parties an ongoing rate for these services but decided to make it free, with only a RMB300 (US$48 in 2013) certification fee to verify the identity of the party. Gerald Hu, Head of Business of WeChat Open Platforms, recalled: "They said we were 'buddha-like' in that we were helping others... but we saw it like honeybees that will benefit from the honey that pollinates the flowers."[89]

In the next stage, Official Accounts were created that enabled brands and businesses to have direct contact with their consumers in WeChat, communicating straight to them about the brand's products and services. By the end of 2014, there were 8 million Official Accounts on WeChat.[90] It was an easy place for consumers to look up a fitness centre's schedule or to find out that their favourite clothing shop was running a seasonal promotion. By the end of 2016, with all these innovations and a high-functioning ecosystem of utility for users, WeChat's monthly active users exploded to close to 900m,[91] an astounding 5-year growth trajectory that was unparalleled in the history of apps anywhere in the world. By 2016, WeChat was also present outside of China, used in Southeast Asia, India and Latin America, as well as many places where Chinese residents or tourists could be found. WeChat scan codes for payment were as likely to be found in branded luxury stores in New York City or London as they were in Shanghai or Guangzhou.

In 2017, in the third stage of development, WeChat launched Mini-Programs. Mini-Programs are sub-applications, or an app within an app, for businesses to run directly in the WeChat app, with WeChat Pay frictionlessly linked. On Mini-Programs, groceries can be ordered from Aldi or pizza from Pizza Hut; clothing from Lululemon or Zara; makeup and toiletries from Sephora and Watsons; fitness classes or doctor's appointments can be booked and more. What is particularly interesting about WeChat Mini-Programs is how small businesses and entrepreneurs leveraged this function as a turnkey e-commerce solution. Mini-Programs had great utility for these businesses, cutting out the need for distributors and giving them a direct-to-consumer (DTC) channel for sales, as well as a platform where they could engage consumers in chat, provide customer service, distribute advertising and other service messages, thus making a business's Mini-Program a fully functioning selling and communications channel. Mini-Programs were easier to build and could be created for about 20% of the cost of a standalone app.[92] Furthermore, they didn't require the user to download, install and register – all the necessary information was carried over from WeChat, and payment was enabled by WeChat Pay. Users could just use the Mini-Program and leave it without yet another app cluttering their phone.

Allen Zhang spoke about the power of the platform in 2019: "WeChat's driving force can be summarized in two points… First, to create a good tool that can keep up with the times… the second driving force is to let creators cultivate value. After the Official Accounts platform got started, WeChat began to reflect the advantages of being a platform, later including Mini-Programs. When a platform only focuses on pursuing its own benefits, it won't last. When a platform creates benefits for others, it takes on a life of its own…. A lot of people do not understand why Mini-Programs are decentralized. If we didn't decentralize it, Tencent could monopolize the platform with its own Mini-Programs and there would be no external developers. Sure, Tencent would benefit in the short term, but the platform ecosystem would not."

It is estimated that by building a powerful value constellation for users with an ecosystem of services and providers through Official Account and Mini-Programs, WeChat created 22.35m job opportunities in 2018 alone.[93]

WeChat has put the user experience first and in doing so has created an ecosystem with an enormous amount of value for its partner businesses and brands. Rather than just offer advertising, which in fact is minimal on the app relative to other social and e-commerce apps globally, they created a powerful ecosystem where businesses could sell direct to consumers, and own and manage their relationship with customers, creating a frictionless experience for both the businesses and users to access the goods and services they need for their daily lives. Zhang noted in 2019: "WeChat has reached one billion users, but actually we've never thought that the number of users was particularly important... we care more about how to provide our users with more services. This is a more important question."[94]

Despite the sprawling digital ecosystem that WeChat was becoming, founder Zhang always insisted that navigation be super simple from the beginning: "WeChat shall always have a four-icon bar, and never add anything to it."[95] Despite the increasing complexity of features, payments, Mini-Programs and more, the four-icon bar remains unchanged even today, which means the development team must continually find other ways to solve for user navigation of the super app.

The digital ecosystem that WeChat has created continues to scale and grow, with seemingly limitless potential. Performance metrics are eye-popping:

- By the end of 2021, there were 450m daily active users of WeChat Mini-Programs, a 15.2% growth from the year prior,[96] which the company believes is a key reason monthly active users grow as well – as utility increases, so does the user base.

- As of March 2023, the monthly active users of WeChat globally have increased another 30%, reaching 1.3bn.

- The number of Mini-Programs by overseas merchants grew by 268% over the past two years, with online commerce transaction volume exploding by 897%.[97]

- Monthly active users of WeChat Search jumped to 700 million in 2021, up 40% from a year ago.[98]

- WeChat Pay employees have grown threefold since 2016, reaching 1,200 people, with the service now featuring more than 1,800 bank and financial institution partners.[99]

- Livestreaming e-commerce sales on WeChat grew by 15 times in 2021.[100]

- WeChat's WeCom, launched in 2016, the enterprise version of the app intended to support businesses in digital transformation with video streaming, communication and messaging services, reached over 180m active users with more than 10m companies in 2021.[101]

By assembling such a powerful ecosystem of value for users, WeChat has effectively become the operating system of daily life in China, used by 80% of the population and occupying 30% of the time people spend on their phones.[102] WeChat's reach outside of China continues to grow too, with users predominantly in Asia; venture capitalists and investors report that WeChat is a model that innovators in India and Africa are trying to learn from in order to potentially transform their own societies and economies.

Indeed, WeChat represents a level of unparalleled utility for both businesses and consumers. The WeChat ecosystem generates a vast amount of user data, enabling businesses to gain valuable insights into consumer behaviour, preferences and trends. This data-driven approach empowers companies to make informed decisions and optimize their products and services. Use cases are seemingly endless. User behaviour analysis yields valuable insights into how users engage with content, products, and services and how users navigate their offer. This is tremendously useful to businesses, helping them to make data-driven decisions to optimize their strategies and offerings. Marketing can be precision-targeted, going after increasingly specific audiences with potentially narrow interests, but with a more relevant offer. This level of personalization benefits both consumers and marketers in bringing the right products to the right audiences with a high degree of efficiency. In fact, by analyzing usage data, businesses can identify areas for improvement, understand user pain points, and gather feedback on new features or offerings to create even better and more tailored products and services that better meet consumers' needs. Further, WeChat's data enables businesses to build and maintain strong customer relationships. By understanding user interactions and preferences, businesses can provide personalized customer support, offer timely promotions, and address individual needs effectively. This data-driven approach helps in enhancing customer satisfaction, loyalty and retention.

ASSEMBLING ECOSYSTEMS OF VALUE MAY BE CLOSER THAN WE THINK

WeChat as a super-app is a potential model for the world for how to assemble meaningful ecosystems of value. What is often overlooked in examining WeChat as a model is that none of this was new technology. In fact, no invention or particular technological breakthrough enabled WeChat to become the essential super-app in China that it is today. Instead, Tencent cobbled together existing tools, technologies and functionality to create something more valuable than any of those components individually. Thus, in looking to create ecosystems of value that unlock progress for both business and consumers, businesses potentially need look no further than what exists today and how combinations thereof can be reimagined into a whole that is greater than the sum of its parts. New realities may be closer at hand than we ever dreamed.

Chapter 7

Marketing, Design and Creativity with AI

The world of creative output, digital marketing and social commerce is on the brink of an exciting revolution, fuelled by the growing influence of artificial intelligence. Technology has already transformed many aspects of this field, replacing traditional practices with computer graphics, software macros and filters. However, AI is set to take this transformation to a whole new level, unlocking opportunities for brands, agencies and creative talent that were previously unimaginable.

One of the most striking aspects of this transformation is the way in which AI-powered design tools are now enhancing the creative output from familiar software. Much of what took many man-hours – product photography, retouching of photographs, location shooting, styling and makeup – has been replaced by computer graphics technology, software macros and shortcuts, and filters. Design software such as Adobe Creative Suite, Canva and Sketch have democratized design by significantly simplifying the creation of high-quality graphics such as logos and other visual design content, meaning anyone can create their own website or brand visual identity in an afternoon instead of weeks or months of effort.

For years, shooting on green screens allowed us to portray scenes seemingly taking place on the moon or on the streets of Paris from studios in London or Los Angeles. Advanced 3D rendering technology has now enabled us to create realistic representations of products that look like photographic images, but for a fraction of the time and price of product photography shoots – no elaborate shooting crews or lighting equipment, just a day of a skilled 3D designer's time.

Large advertising and media buying teams have been replaced by automated advertising platforms. Google Ads and Facebook ads make it easier for marketers to forgo agencies altogether and create and run their own campaigns, and social media management tools help manage and schedule posts, track engagement and analyze performance.

With the help of augmented reality beauty filters, digital influencers look like they just stepped out of a makeup artist's chair, enabling them to be camera-ready and shoot anytime, anywhere.

The advent of technology has clearly facilitated a reduction in barriers to commerce, creativity and marketing. With the rise of AI, we are no longer required to have knowledge of computer programming to utilize its capabilities. AI has the ability to automate tasks, analyze data and personalize content, and this has the potential to transform the way brands, agencies and creative talent create and distribute digital content.

AI-powered design tools take the output of conventional software to new heights, expanding the boundaries of what seems to be the realm of science fiction. The use of generative adversarial networks (GANs), for example, allows for the development of entirely new and unique designs. This is achieved by pitting two neural networks against each other; one generates images, while the other seeks to determine if these images are genuine or fake. This process leads to the creation of unique designs never seen before, which can be applied in various areas, including advertising and marketing.

AI is also changing the game in content personalization. With the vast amounts of data available through social media, search engines and other online platforms, AI algorithms can analyze user behaviour to create content tailored to individual users. This ranges from personalized product recommendations on e-commerce sites to customized social media feeds based on individual preferences and interests. Research shows that personalized content is more likely to be engaged with and shared than generic content, making it one of the most effective ways to increase audience engagement and brand awareness.

AI has already propelled platforms such as Google Ads and Facebook ads to greater heights of automation. These platforms use machine learning algorithms to enhance ad performance, allowing them to analyze data on user behaviour, ad performance and other factors to constantly optimize ad targeting and placement.

Chatbots and virtual assistants powered by AI are becoming increasingly popular too, providing customers with instant access to information and support. These tools are not only useful for customer service but also for marketing purposes, enabling businesses to engage with customers in a more personalized and effective way in real time, without the need to wait to engage a human being for support during limited business hours.

GENERATIVE ADVERSARIAL NETWORKS (GANs) PUSH CREATIVE BOUNDARIES

As mentioned earlier, GANs are a type of neural network architecture used in unsupervised machine learning. GANs consist of two neural networks – a generator and a discriminator – that are trained together to generate new and unique data. The generator network is tasked with creating new data that mimics a given dataset, while the discriminator network's job is to identify whether the generated data is real or fake. During training, the two networks are pitted against each other, with the generator trying to produce data that can fool the discriminator into thinking it is real. As training progresses, both networks get better at their respective tasks, and the generator learns to create more and more realistic data.

GANs have been used in a variety of applications, including image and video generation, data augmentation, and data synthesis. For instance, GANs are used to create realistic images of human faces, which can be useful in fields like computer vision and facial recognition. In addition, GANs can be used to generate new data from existing datasets, which is helpful in situations where data is limited or expensive to obtain. GANs are most familiar to some as they have come to be known in some cases as "deep fakes".

A deep fake involves taking a video of a person and using deep learning algorithms to modify it in a way that makes the person appear to be saying or doing something that they didn't actually say or do. For example, a deep fake video could be created that shows a politician giving a speech that they never actually gave, or a celebrity engaging in behaviour that they never actually engaged in. Deep fakes can involve face swapping, voice cloning and synthetic generation. They have become a growing concern in recent years as they can be used for malicious purposes such as spreading false information, defaming individuals and manipulating public opinion. Also, there is the potential for copyright issues with celebrity talent being "cast" into videos they never agreed to be in.

There have been several high-profile deep fakes that gained widespread attention and went viral. One example was a deep fake video of Barack Obama, created by comedian Jordan Peele, that went viral in 2018. The video showed Obama delivering a PSA about the dangers of deep fakes and was intended to raise awareness about the technology. In 2019, an artist created a deep fake video of Facebook CEO Mark Zuckerberg, showing him giving a speech about the power of Facebook and its influence on society. The video was intended to criticize Zuckerberg and highlight the potential dangers of social media. Yet another viral deep fake was of Tom Cruise on TikTok in 2021. The video showed a person who appeared to be Tom Cruise performing various stunts and magic tricks. And then there have been deep fakes of Marilyn Monroe and Elvis and more celebrities who are no longer with us, with the deep fakes imagining what they might have said or done in various modern scenarios in today's world.

Outside of the more well-known and viral examples of GANs in deep fakes, there are companies and organizations that use GANs successfully in business applications. One of the most well-known companies that uses GANs is NVIDIA, a technology company developing graphics processing units (GPUs) for computers and other devices. NVIDIA has developed a number of GAN models, including StyleGAN and StyleGAN2, which are used for generating high-quality images of people, animals and other objects. These models have been used in a variety of applications, including art, fashion and advertising.

GANs have been used in fashion to generate new and unique designs. Fast-fashion brands such as H&M and Zara are particularly well suited to experiment with a GAN-based system for generating whole new collections of clothing. GANs can start by generating new designs based on existing style inspirations, and then these new designs can be evaluated by a team of fashion experts who are able to use their expertise to select the most promising designs and refine them further – resulting in a whole collection of new and unique designs. By using GANs to generate new designs, brands reduce the time and cost associated with traditional design processes, making fast fashion even faster. Because GAN-based systems are able to generate new-to-the-world designs quickly and efficiently, this allows the team to focus on refining the most promising designs and bringing them to market. Additionally, the use of GANs allows businesses to generate new and unique designs that were not possible with traditional design processes. This serves to help fast-fashion brands to not only push the creative envelope in design, but also to differentiate their products in a competitive fashion market and capture consumers looking for out-of-the-box, innovative designs.

Another example of high-potential application is the gaming industry, where GANs have been used to create realistic images of game characters and environments. In 2020, the gaming company Square Enix used a GAN-based system to create a realistic 3D model of the character Aerith Gainsborough from its popular game Final Fantasy VII. The system used a GAN to generate new images of Aerith based on existing images, which were then used to create a 3D model of the character. The result was a highly detailed and super-realistic model that was used in the game's remake to bring the character to life in a way that was not possible with traditional animation techniques. In this way, any celebrity, politician, or even an ordinary individual could become the hero of their own video game.

Google has used the technology to create realistic images of landmarks and to enhance the quality of low-resolution images. Google has also used GANs in its Google Photos service to create animations and collages. Other companies and organizations that use GANs include Facebook, which uses the technology for image and video processing, and OpenAI, a research organization that focuses on artificial intelligence and machine learning. GANs are becoming increasingly popular as a way to generate new and unique data, and we can expect to see more companies and organizations using GANs and other machine learning techniques in the future.

One particularly imaginative application was seen recently in China. In 2023, it was reported that some Chinese funeral homes were using the technology is offer "digital immortality" packages as part of their funeral services.[103] Specifically, they use AI and machine learning algorithms such as GANs to simulate the deceased's personality, behaviour and expressions. With just a few inputs provided by the family, a virtual version of the deceased can appear on video and have simple conversations in their own voice with the family members after they have passed away. The belief is that this will help in the grieving process, even allowing family members who are not present to find closure.

And this is just the beginning. While GANs are now being applied in a variety of industries to improve and enhance existing products and services, we can expect entirely new and wildly imaginative new services and use cases in the very near future.

AN AI-POWERED MARKETING AGENCY

Based in Shanghai, Tezign is a marketing solutions agency that provides a range of marketing, advertising, design and digital services – all powered by AI. The company was founded in 2014 by a group of designers and entrepreneurs with the aim of providing innovative design solutions leveraging the latest in AI technology. The name itself is inspired by the mashup of "tech" plus "design". Tezign has over 1,000 local and multinational clients across a range of industries, including technology, finance, healthcare, consumer products and education, and has won prestigious design awards for their work.

Tezign leverages AI in multiple ways to work more efficiently and at a lower cost base than the traditional agency model. AI is cleverly utilized to automate repetitive design tasks which typically are resource-heavy but low-margin in traditional agencies, such as resizing images or creating variations of a design in different formats for different uses, e.g. cutting a 6-second social commerce video down to a 3-second social media post. Tezign also uses AI-powered image recognition to automatically tag and categorize images in large databases. This helps designers quickly find the images they need for a project, saving time and improving accuracy. These simplified, automated tasks allow designers to focus on more complex and creative tasks, leading to more efficient and effective workflows. Designers get to move upstream to focus on the creative concepts instead of being bogged down in the execution.

Additionally, Tezign uses AI to analyze user behaviour data to optimize user experience (UX) design. By analyzing how users interact with websites or apps, Tezign can identify areas for improvement and make data-driven design decisions to improve the customer experience. AI is also used in predictive analytics to analyze user data and predict future trends. This helps designers create designs that are more likely to resonate with target audiences, improving the effectiveness of marketing campaigns and other digital initiatives.

And it's not just the creative process that is optimized. AI also supports how Tezign works with its clients. A matching algorithm and image recognition system matches designers with clients based on the client's project brief and needs, quickly building a fit-for-purpose team that can be instantly activated. Further, AI-powered chatbots and virtual assistants provide customer support and streamline communication with clients, handling simple inquiries and requests, freeing up Tezign employees' time to focus on more high-level tasks.

To give an idea of Tezign's work, here are some examples of their projects:

- WeChat Mini-Programs: Tezign was responsible for designing the user interface and user experience for WeChat's Mini-Programs, which are lightweight, e-commerce-enabled apps that can be accessed within the WeChat platform. Tezign's work helped to make the Mini-Programs user-friendly and intuitive and one of the best-performing social commerce platforms.

- Huawei P9 Leica Dual-Camera Smartphone: Tezign designed the campaign and messaging for Huawei's P9 smartphone, which highlighted the camera's dual-lens technology. The campaign was a huge success and helped to establish Huawei as a major player in the smartphone industry.

- BMW X5: Tezign designed a variety of dynamic visual elements for BMW's X5 campaign, which emphasized the vehicle's power and performance, helping to increase sales of the X5 and solidify BMW's position in the luxury car market in China.

- DiDi App: Tezign was responsible for designing the app user interface and user experience for DiDi Chuxing, the largest ride-hailing platform in China. Tezign's work helped to make the app easy to use and contributed to its popularity and eventual dominance in the transport and ride-sharing space.

- Coca-Cola: Tezign designed the packaging and graphic visual elements for Coca-Cola's "Share a Coke" campaign in China for hundreds of individually designed cans of Coke. This wide range of personalized cans encouraged people to share a Coke with friends and loved ones. The campaign was regarded as a big success and helped to significantly increase Coca-Cola sales in China.

And this is just the beginning. Tezign's aim is to rethink design entirely, and it has started a research lab at Tongji University in collaboration with Alibaba. The Design and Artificial Intelligence Lab's goal is to test how data, the internet, machine learning and algorithms can reimagine design as a profession and a service. In 2017 the lab issued its first Design and Artificial Intelligence Report, which had over 100,000 downloads in the first six months.[104] In the same year, the lab produced its first project: Luban, an AI-assisted banner-generation software. During the 11/11 Chinese sales festival, Luban generated 170 million online banners. Tezign Founder and CEO Fan Ling remarked, "Imagine that a human designer produced each banner worth at least RMB20 to RMB100, multiply that by 170 million, and that's a huge amount of revenue. With that amount of banners, you can push not only different products, but also different brand information to different consumers. I believe this can massively increase the consumer engagement rate."[105]

Tezign has attracted a series of high-profile investors and over $100m in funding from the likes of Singapore's Temasek Holdings, Sequoia Capital, Hearst, SoftBank Venture Capital and more.[106] Based on the company's current trajectory and recent developments in the design and technology industries, expect Tezign to continue to redefine the future of creativity and marketing services with the application of emerging technologies.

LARGE LANGUAGE MODELS' POTENTIAL TO TRANSFORM MARKETING AND CREATIVITY

Large language models such as Generative Pre-trained Transformers (GPT) have already made significant advancements in the fields of marketing, creative and content development, and the future looks very promising. Across e-commerce, entertainment and education, GPTs are being used to create personalized content for individuals based on their preferences, history and behaviour. What is now emerging is the technology trajectory for large language models to be an inspiring collaborator and tool in these fields.

For example, GPTs can help creators in fields such as music, writing and art by assisting in the generation of new ideas, improving workflow and generating content that can be used as a starting point for further creativity. GPTs can also be used to facilitate collaboration between creators, allowing them to work together more efficiently and effectively. This can be especially useful in fields such as filmmaking, where multiple artists must work together to create a final product. Further, GPTs can be used to automate certain tasks in the creative and content development process, such as generating on-trend social media posts or summarizing long articles into bite-sized key points. This can save creators time and allow them to focus on more challenging and creative tasks, effectively enabling them to move upstream to prioritize pure human creativity and ideas over execution and operational details. With that in mind, both the potential for efficiencies and cost savings, as well as the uplevelling of human productivity and creativity, is staggering.

In fact, there are a great many use cases that can streamline the level of human involvement required in content development. This is because GPTs can produce content at a much faster rate than humans, saving time and labour in the content creation process. For example, a GPT tool can generate thousands of product descriptions in minutes, while it may take human writers days or weeks to complete the same task. GPTs can automate repetitive and mundane tasks, such as data analysis and keyword research, allowing content creators to focus on more creative and high-value work, increasing efficiency and saving time in the production process.

Also, social channels can be managed by AI and GPTs – a task usually handled by teams of social media marketers. Hootsuite, a social media management platform, uses generative AI to automate social media tasks and improve social media performance for businesses of all sizes. Hootsuite's AI-powered features include automated scheduling, content curation, and post recommendations. The platform analyzes data from social media channels to identify the best times to post, the types of content that resonate with the audience, and the hashtags that generate the most engagement. Based on this analysis, Hootsuite's generative AI can then make recommendations on what content to post, when to post it, and what hashtags to use. The reduction in time and cost is particularly beneficial for businesses with limited resources, and can serve to level the playing field, thereby enabling smaller businesses to be more competitive and have a more impactful presence with their potential customers. Of course, these systems need humans to run them and to be the quality control and ultimate curator of content, but imagine that perhaps one person could be running several social accounts rather than just one, which creates a whole new level of productivity and income potential for the individual.

GPTs can also produce quality content that meets highly specific standards and requirements. For example, an AI tool can generate content that is optimized for SEO or conforms to a specific style guide. It can even adapt and prepare materials for a variety of geographies and languages, making global launches faster and more streamlined. Rather than a complex, staged rollout, imagine a simultaneous global launch made easy with generative AI.

It is important to reiterate here that the use of generative AI does not eliminate the need for human involvement or oversight. The technology is still evolving and may not always produce the desired results. However, with human steering and curation, it can help a team move at hyper-speed, and significantly reduce time and costs.

GROUNDBREAKING AI APPLICATIONS AND USE CASES

Today, AI is unleashing new use cases every day, a great many of these helping to propel human creativity to the next level. For example, the AI-powered art platform ArtBreeder allows users to create a unique and original art style by combining different techniques and characteristics to generate novel ideas and inspirational starting points for new work. AI-powered music composition tools, such as Amper Music, generate custom-made music tracks based on a user's input, such as genre, tempo and mood. It has been used by musicians, filmmakers and game developers to create original soundtracks. AI-powered game engines, such as Unity and Unreal Engine, can generate game assets such as characters, environments and animations, reducing the detailed executional workload of game developers, enabling them to spend more time on scenario ideation. Additionally, AI can be used to create procedurally generated content, such as levels and maps, enhancing the gameplay experience. Even AI-powered content optimization tools, such as MarketMuse, can analyze content for SEO and make suggestions for improving relevance and quality, leading to improved content and increased online visibility.

Beyond digital platforms, AI is also being used to generate innovation and creativity in centuries-old industries such as beer brewing. For example, at Molson Coors-owned, Detroit-based Atwater Brewing, an AI-created recipe gave birth to a new beer in 2023: Artificial Intelligence IPA. The recipe was developed by a quality assurance manager who was playing with ChatGPT and asked it to come up with a recipe for an IPA beer. The prompt was to create a recipe based on the specific hops that were in Atwater's inventory. When ChatGPT delivered a home-brew-scale recipe, it was then asked to scale this to 20 barrels, to fit the exact size of the Atwater facility. Atwater followed the resulting recipe and successfully launched the product in its taprooms shortly thereafter.

In publishing, the *Washington Post* has been using AI in the form of their AI-powered tool Heliograf, which generates news articles on specific topics such as sports, politics and weather. Heliograf uses Natural Language Processing (NLP) and machine learning algorithms to analyze data sources, such as social media and government reports, and then generates news articles in real-time. One of the key benefits of Heliograf is its ability to generate news stories more quickly than a typical newsroom operation can. For example, in a recent US Presidential election, Heliograf generated more than 500 articles in just a few months, covering topics such as election results and polling data. These articles were published on the paper's website and mobile app, providing readers with up-to-date and relevant news content. Heliograf is also able to personalize content for readers. It can analyze readers' behaviour and interests, and then generate news articles that are tailored to their preferences, leading to increased reader engagement and retention – an advantage in the highly competitive media industry.

In marketing and advertising, AI is being used to dramatically step-change communication effectiveness through personalization. Burger King was extremely progressive in 2019 when it experimented with AI to create a unique marketing campaign for their Whopper in Brazil. They decided to leverage generative AI to create personalized ads that would reflect the unique taste preferences of each customer. To do this, Burger King partnered with the Brazilian ad agency David Sao Paulo, and used an AI-powered tool called "The Whopper Recommender". This tool analyzed data from Burger King's loyalty programme, including customers' past orders and food preferences, and then generated personalized recommendations for each customer. The recommendations were then used to create personalized ads that were served to customers on Burger King's website and mobile app. The ads featured images and descriptions of customized Whopper sandwiches based on the customer's taste preferences, such as extra cheese or spicy sauce. The campaign was a huge success, with a 45% increase in Whopper sales during the first month of the campaign. The personalized ads had a clickthrough rate of 27%, which was significantly higher than Burger King's previous campaigns, demonstrating the potential of generative AI in marketing, particularly in industries where personalization and customization are key factors in customer engagement and retention.

And in executive management, in what might be viewed as a publicity stunt more than a strategic business decision, a publicly traded company in China has appointed an AI CEO. NetDragon Websoft is a technology company listed on the Hong Kong Stock Exchange that specializes in developing and publishing online games and mobile apps, including popular titles such as Conquer Online, Eudemons Online and Heroes Evolved. The company has also developed educational software for primary and secondary schools which are widely used in China. In recent years, NetDragon Websoft has been investing heavily in AI and VR technologies, establishing a research and development centre and launching several products, such as an AI-powered online classroom and a VR-enhanced online shopping platform. In August 2020, the company appointed Tang Yu, an AI-powered virtual humanoid robot, as its CEO.

CEO Tang Yu is not a fully autonomous AI system that makes high-level decisions on its own. Instead, it serves as a tool to assist human executives in their decision-making process by providing data and analysis. NetDragon Websoft has stated that the virtual CEO is intended to be a symbol of the company's commitment to AI and innovation. And while it is not possible to directly attribute business results to Tang Yu's recommendations, actions or decisions, it should be noted that NetDragon Websoft reported solid financial results for the year 2020. The company's revenue for 2020 increased by 7.8% year-on-year to RMB9.1bn (US$1.4bn), and its net profit increased by 20.4% year-on-year to RMB1.4bn (US$212m).[107] This has bolstered the company's stock performance as well, increasing its share price by 10% and outperforming the Hang Seng Index, the index that tracks the largest companies listed on the Hong Kong Stock Exchange.[108]

GENERATIVE AI: NEAR-FUTURE IMPACT IN BUSINESS

Generative AI at its current level of development feels in many ways like the World Wide Web in the early 1990s. The technology is still nascent but those who can imagine its expanded use cases believe it will be equivalent in impact to the internet and at the centre of a fourth industrial revolution. Some predictions on where it is headed in the near future include:

- Improved Natural Language Processing: NLP is a crucial component of generative AI, as it enables machines to understand and generate human-like language. We can expect to see significant advancements in NLP, including better language understanding, more accurate translations, and improved natural language generation, leading to use applications such as script and dialogue writing, email writing and response automation, and broad customer service applications.

- Micro-personalization: We can expect to see even greater levels of personalization across marketing, content creation and customer service, which will allow businesses to tailor their products and services at potentially a one-to-one and individual level, leading to increased customer satisfaction and loyalty via bespoke offers.

- Automation as a new standard: Generative AI has already proven to be a valuable tool for automating repetitive tasks, such as content creation and social media management. In the future, we can expect to see even greater levels of automation, particularly in industries such as manufacturing, logistics and transportation.

- Advancements in computer vision: Computer vision enables machines to "see" and understand visual data. In the future, we can expect significant advancements in computer vision, including improved object recognition, enhanced 3D modelling, and better image and video analysis, which could transform industries from filmmaking and entertainment to policing and security.

Of course, the rise of AI also raises concerns about job destruction and human obsolescence in certain types of work. As AI continues to automate tasks previously performed by humans, it is true than some tasks currently done by humans may become obsolete. However, this is not unlike the era of automation in industrial manufacturing which displaced a great deal of lower-value manual labour and led to a great awakening in human and economic productivity globally.

And while AI has the potential to automate many tasks, it should be noted that the technology is currently reliant on human input and collaboration. It is likely that we will not see AI totally replacing humans across vast swaths of industry as some concerned voices seem to suggest today, but rather more likely is AI assisting humans to become more productive and collaborative as execution becomes automated. Further, new jobs within AI will also emerge. For example, we see even in recent months roles like ChatGPT Prompt Engineer being created – because the best answers from ChatGPT come from the best and most cleverly structured prompts. The prevailing wisdom of the moment suggests that while AI will not replace humans, humans who use AI will replace those who do not.

Writer's Note

This last chapter on generative AI was written with assistance from ChatGPT. Based on my own knowledge and previous research on AI and generative AI, I created and provided the prompts that formed the basis of my research for this chapter in the book.

My observation in using ChatGPT in this fashion was that it didn't necessarily change my thinking or approach to writing, but it did make the process much faster. Typically, even as a subject matter expert, it can still take weeks or months to write and research an example or a case study-driven chapter for a business book. I estimate that ChatGPT cut my research time by two-thirds. I used it both to research cases that I already knew about and to find cases that I was previously unaware of. I asked it to provide sources for the examples and used the examples from the most robust sources – generally from well-respected, well-known global or national press and media outlets and publishers. It was, in some ways, like having a human research assistant.

To give a behind-the-scenes peek, I will share with you some of the ChatGPT prompts. I knew what I wanted to talk about, and so my prompts were structured accordingly. Here are some of the specific prompts for reference:

- What is the future of generative AI for creative and content development?

- Please provide some case studies or examples of using generative AI to manage social platforms for small businesses.

- Tell me more about GANs and how they have been used or can be used by businesses or brands in marketing to generate new outcomes.

- What do clients say about working with Tezign over traditional agencies? Who has invested in Tezign?

- Tell me more about Tang Yu, the AI CEO of NetDragon Websoft. Describe the company, how it works to have

an AI CEO, and what business results can be attributed to this novel approach.

Once I obtained and checked the research, I then adapted the
information and text that ChatGPT provided into my own style,
tweaking some of the language, restructuring sentences, and
reordering information to tell the stories of business in the
way I preferred to narrate them. By saving so much time in the
research phase, overall the time spent writing this chapter was
about half that of other chapters in the book of the same length
and depth.

Reader, what do you think? Was the depth of information, the
tone, voice or presentation of this chapter markedly different
from the others? Did you perceive a different type of engagement while reading this chapter? How do you feel now knowing
the chapter was ChatGPT-assisted?

Chapter 8

Conclusion: The Future is Already Here

In William Gibson's 1984 science fiction novel *Neuromancer*, a down-on-his-luck cyberhacker hired for one last job faces off with an intelligent computer. Gibson, who popularized the term "cyberspace", is well known for predicting technologies and innovations in his books that are somehow just around the corner. When asked by *The Economist* in 2003 how he predicted artificial intelligence in 1984 when computers were not even yet widely prevalent, Gibson quipped, "The future is already here, it is just very unevenly distributed."

Gibson's sentiment is that invention, innovation and progress are happening all around us; they are just not always visible from where we might personally sit. Further, if we dig into these pockets, we can crystal-ball-gaze and somewhat reliably predict the future. Imagine... somewhere in the world, there are pockets of innovation we do not see, with people designing futures filled with technologies and experiences we cannot imagine, be it in a lab in Mumbai, a conference room in Silicon Valley, an office in London, or in someone's garage in a nondescript small US town.

In principle, the ideas and innovations with potential take hold, and like seeds are propagated and grow. If they are significant and game-changing enough, these seeds spread widely and have global reach and impact. Then later, for those who might not have a bird's-eye view on their isolated beginnings, these innovations seemingly rise from nowhere.

Take ChatGPT, for example. Based on the recent hype and buzz around large language model AI systems like ChatGPT, some might perceive AI as having only recently burst onto the scene. However, AI was established as an academic discipline in 1956 at the Dartmouth Conference, following McCulloch and Pitts' 1942 model of an artificial neuron (a fundamental precursor to neural networks) as well as Alan Turing's famous "Turing Test" in 1950, which measured a machine's ability to exhibit intelligent behaviour that was indistinguishable from that of a human.[109] So the idea of AI as a recent technology is a false notion. More accurately, we are just now becoming hyper-aware of AI as it has now reached the level of development where it will undoubtedly reshape our industries, our daily life and our societies – but in reality, in some corners of the world, people have been quietly progressing on AI for more than 70 years.

So today, when we scan the horizons for weak signals of what the future of marketing may look like, we will no doubt look to technology giants in Silicon Valley and to creative agencies in bustling metropolises like New York and London. However, it's not just the well-established centres of innovation that are shaping the future of marketing; there are countless emerging hotspots where groundbreaking ideas are being conceived and brought to life. Within the context of this book, many China examples have been given, and China is indeed one of the markets to watch for technology that has high potential for commercial and marketing application.

Another such hub is nestled in the heart of Mumbai, India. A vibrant city teeming with energy and entrepreneurial spirit, Mumbai has become a breeding ground for technological advancements that are revolutionizing the marketing landscape. In the bustling offices of startups and research institutions, a new wave of AI-driven marketing solutions is taking shape. From predictive analytics algorithms that anticipate consumer behaviour to personalized advertising platforms that dynamically adapt to individual preferences, Mumbai's innovators are at the forefront of marrying technology and marketing in unprecedented ways.

Meanwhile, as post-COVID tech workers redistribute to living in small American towns with lower costs of living, clusters of passionate individuals in Texas and Idaho are fusing art and technology to redefine the boundaries of experiential marketing. Armed with a diverse skillset and a shared vision, these self-proclaimed "garage innovators" are creating immersive brand experiences that blur the lines between the physical and digital realms. Through the use of augmented and virtual reality, they are transporting consumers into captivating narratives that leave lasting impressions and forge deep connections with brands.

And of course, in the boardrooms of established companies and the incubators of ambitious startups, the future of marketing is being shaped. In London, renowned for its creative prowess, teams of marketers are collaborating with data scientists and psychologists to unlock the secrets of consumer decision-making.

By delving into the depths of human cognition and emotion, they are crafting persuasive messaging that resonates with audiences on a profound level, fostering brand loyalty and advocacy.

Our global ability for interconnectedness has the potential to accelerate the exchange of ideas between these hubs and propel advancements forward. Innovations that originate in Mumbai can find their way to London, while breakthroughs emerging from Silicon Valley can permeate global markets. The collective intelligence and collaboration across borders is poised to combine to create a rich ecosystem where the seeds of innovation spread rapidly, transcending geographical boundaries and igniting change on a global scale. This interconnectedness of our modern world will have the future impact of speeding up the lag time between inventions and their eventual game-changing applications.

And as the convergence of these forces presents marketers with unparalleled opportunities to connect with consumers in meaningful ways, there are most certainly future outcomes that are currently unimaginable. We find ourselves standing on the cusp of a new era. The rapid advancement of technology and exponential growth of AI have forever altered the landscape of marketing. Marketers now wield powerful tools that can analyze vast amounts of data, predict consumer behaviour, and personalize experiences on an unprecedented scale, rendering them seemingly omniscient about what consumers want, why they want it, and how they want it.

CMOs WILL BECOME LARGER BUYERS OF TECHNOLOGY THAN CIOs

In this evolving landscape of marketing, where technology is the driving force behind innovation and transformation, a notable shift is taking place. It is predicted that Chief Marketing Officers (CMOs) will become increasingly significant buyers of technology, surpassing the traditional role of Chief Information Officers (CIOs) as the key organizational buyers of technology in companies. This shift represents a fundamental change in the hierarchy of technology decision-making within organizations and reflects the growing influence of marketing in the digital age.

Historically, CIOs have held the reins when it comes to technology procurement and implementation and their primary focus has been on the infrastructure, security and operational aspects of technology within an organization. CIOs have played a critical role in companies to ensure that the business's technology systems are robust, scalable and compliant with local laws and regulations. However, as the marketing landscape continues to evolve, marketing has transcended its traditional boundaries and become deeply intertwined with technology and data-driven insights. In the digital marketing age, CMOs are taking on a more strategic role in driving business growth, and as a result, driving successful marketing strategies heavily relies on leveraging advanced technologies and harnessing the power of data analytics. Today, CMOs must be at the forefront of technology adoption and innovation, embracing emerging technologies such as AI, machine learning, big data analytics and marketing automation, in order to gain a competitive edge.

Another factor contributing to the increased role of CMOs in technology decision-making is the growing importance of customer experience. In today's competitive landscape, delivering exceptional customer experiences has become a key differentiator for businesses. Customer expectations have evolved, and consumers now demand seamless, personalized interactions across multiple touchpoints. Technology plays a pivotal role in enabling businesses to meet these elevated customer expectations. From marketing automation platforms that enable personalized messaging to customer relationship management (CRM) systems that centralize customer data, technology solutions are essential in creating and delivering outstanding customer experiences. CMOs, who are responsible for driving customer-centric strategies, are in a prime position to identify and implement the technology solutions that facilitate exceptional experiences throughout the customer journey.

Today's organizations have access to vast amounts of consumer data, collected from various touchpoints throughout the ever-evolving customer journey. This data holds valuable insights not only for impactful marketing strategies and enhanced customer experiences, but also for optimized business outcomes. CMOs, armed with their expertise in understanding consumer behaviour and with their finger on the pulse of market trends, are ideally positioned to drive technology investment decisions that go beyond pure marketing efforts. Ideally CMOs and CIOs should partner to invest in advanced marketing technologies, allowing the business to unlock the full potential of their consumer data across the full value chain of the business, thus creating lasting consumer, supplier and partner relationships that form the basis of a strong competitive advantage for the business overall.

A COOKIE-LESS FUTURE WILL ONLY ACCELERATE TECHNOLOGY

A shift to a cookie-less future represents a significant change in the marketing ecosystem, with profound implications for marketers. Cookies, which are small pieces of data stored on users' browsers, have long been a foundational element of digital advertising, enabling personalized targeting and tracking of consumer behaviour. However, as privacy concerns and regulatory measures have escalated, the effectiveness and viability of cookies have come under scrutiny. The regulatory shift towards a cookie-less future will reshape the marketing landscape, and paradoxically, has the potential to make AI and other technologies even more powerful.

One of the key challenges that marketers will face in a cookie-less future is the loss of granular individual-level tracking and targeting. Cookies have allowed marketers to track user behaviour across websites, building comprehensive user profiles and enabling highly targeted advertising campaigns. This level of personalization has been a cornerstone of digital marketing, allowing marketers to deliver relevant content and advertisements to consumers based on their specific interests and preferences. However, with increasing privacy regulations and consumer demands for greater control over their data, major web browsers have implemented changes to limit the effectiveness of third-party cookies, and some have even announced plans to phase them out entirely. In the short term, this means marketers will face new limitations in tracking and targeting individual users across websites.

As such, marketers will need to adapt and find alternative methods to gather insights about their target audiences while respecting privacy boundaries. This is where AI and other technologies come into play, offering solutions that can fill the void left by the diminishing role of cookies. By analyzing large volumes of data, including first-party data, contextual data, and anonymized user information, AI can uncover patterns and insights that were previously derived from individual-level cookie data. AI algorithms can identify clusters of users with similar characteristics and behaviours, allowing marketers to group users based on shared interests or preferences for more effective targeting.

Moreover, AI can enhance the personalization of marketing efforts by generating dynamic content and experiences tailored to specific audience segments. It can analyze user interactions, preferences, and contextual data in real-time to deliver personalized recommendations, product suggestions, or targeted messages, creating a more customized and seamless customer experience than was ever possible with cookies.

In addition to AI, other emerging technologies can also play a crucial role in a cookie-less future. For instance, contextual targeting becomes more valuable in the absence of individual tracking. By analyzing the content, context, and intent of web pages, marketers can deliver ads that are aligned with users' current interests or the content they are consuming at the moment. NLP algorithms can interpret the semantic meaning of text, allowing marketers to understand the context of online conversations and serve up relevant messaging accordingly.

Ultimately, the shift to a cookie-less future emphasizes the importance of building and leveraging first-party data collected directly from consumers – with their consent. By implementing strategies to collect and analyze first-party data, such as through customer relationship management (CRM) systems or loyalty programmes, marketers can gain valuable insights into their customers' preferences, behaviours and purchase history. This data can fuel AI algorithms, enabling marketers to create personalized experiences based on robust and reliable information.

While AI and other technologies can enhance marketing in a cookie-less future, it is essential to balance the power of these technologies with ethical considerations and privacy safeguards. Marketers must prioritize transparency, consent, and data protection to build and maintain trust with consumers.

THE NEW FRONTIER OF MARKETING

Imagine a world where advertisements are no longer interruptions but instead serve as valuable content that enriches the lives of consumers. Through AI-powered algorithms, marketers can decipher the subtle nuances of consumer behaviour, anticipating their needs and desires even before they themselves are fully aware of them. This level of personalization creates a symbiotic relationship between brands and consumers, fostering loyalty and trust.

It is worth noting that the future of marketing is not limited to technology alone. In the pursuit of authenticity and meaningful connections, marketers are rediscovering the power of storytelling. In a world inundated by information, stories have become the currency of attention. Brands that can weave compelling narratives, tapping into the universal human experience, will stand out amidst the noise and forge deep connections with their audiences.

Furthermore, the future of marketing extends beyond the realm of traditional advertising. Influencer marketing, social media, user-generated content and immersive experiences are just a few examples of the evolving landscape. The lines between marketing, entertainment and art continue to blur, giving rise to new and unconventional forms of expression. The marketers of tomorrow must embrace these emerging channels and adapt to the ever-changing preferences and behaviours of consumers.

As we navigate this new frontier, we must acknowledge the ethical implications that arise with the pervasive use of AI in marketing. The power to manipulate and influence consumers is at our fingertips, and it is our responsibility as marketers to wield this power with integrity and transparency. By embracing ethical guidelines and promoting responsible practices, we can ensure that the future of marketing is built on trust and mutual benefit.

In this new era, the key to success lies in embracing change, staying adaptable and maintaining a relentless pursuit of innovation. The seeds of transformation are already sown in the diverse hubs of innovation around the world, waiting to sprout and spread their influence globally. By harnessing the power of technology, embracing the art of storytelling, and doing so with ethical practices, marketers can navigate this ever-changing landscape and create experiences that transcend boundaries.

The future of marketing is already here, and now is the time to seize it. So, let us embark on this journey together, fuelled by curiosity and armed with the tools of tomorrow. Let us seize the opportunities that lie before us, and shape the future of marketing – a future that blends technology and artistry, personalization and authenticity, innovation and a brave new humanity.

Notes

1   Social Commerce Revenue Worldwide from 2022–2030, statista. com, accessed March 17, 2023. Web. https://www.statista.com/ statistics/1231944/social-commerce-global-market-size/#:~:tex- t=Worldwide%2C%20social%20commerce%20generated%20 about,dollars%20in%20the%20latter%20year

2   Jason Davis, "Social Commerce: How Pinduoduo and Instagram Challenge Alibaba and Amazon in Ecommerce," INSEAD Case Study, 2020.

3   Ibid.

4   Ibid.

5   Camilo Becdach, Marc Brodherson, et al., "Social Commerce: The Future of How Consumers Interact with Brands," McKinsey Reports, October 19, 2022, Web. https://www.mckinsey.com/capabilities/ growth-marketing-and-sales/our-insights/social-commerce-the-fu- ture-of-how-consumers-interact-with-brands

6   Yujie Xue, "ByteDance Overtakes AntGroup as the World's Most Valuable Unicorn," South China Morning Post, December 20, 2021. https://www.scmp.com/business/china-business/article/3160424/ bytedance-overtakes-ant-group-worlds-most-valuable-unicorn

7   Roger Chen and Rui Ma, "How ByteDance Became the World's Most Valuable Startup", Harvard Business Review, February 24, 2022.

8   Nessa Anwar, "What is ByteDance?," CNBC, Web. Accessed June 8, 2022. https://www.cnbc.com/2021/11/03/bytedance-founder-zhang- yiming-steps-down-as-chairman-amid-reshuffle.html

9   Pandaily, "TikTok and Sister App Douyin Exceed 3.3 Billion Downloads Worldwide, Generating Nearly 1000 Related Apps", November 25, 2021. Web. https://pandaily.com/tiktok-and-sister-app-douyin-exceed- 3-3-billion-downloads-worldwide-generating-near-1000-related-apps/

10 Russel Flannery, "TikTok's Zhang Yiming's Fortune More Than Doubles as the App's Global Popularity Grows," Forbes, November

3, 2021. https://www.forbes.com/sites/russellflannery/2021/11/03/ tiktoks-zhang-yimings-fortune-more-than-doubles-as-the-apps-global-popularity-grows/?sh=43ef5be23151

11   Isobel Asher Hamilton, "Sheryl Sandberg Says She Worries About TikTok," Business Insider, February 27, 2020. Web. https://www. businessinsider.com/sheryl-sandberg-said-she-worries-about-tiktok-2020-2

12   Paul R. La Monica, "It's Been a Rough Year for Social Media Stocks. Blame TikTok," CNN Business, June 8, 2022. Web.

13   Manish Singh, "Facebook Shutting Down Lasso, It's TikTok Clone," techcrunch.com, July 2, 2020. Web. https://techcrunch.com/2020/07/01/lasso-facebook-tiktok-shut-down/

14   Michael Brennan, Attention Factory, Independently Published, October 10, 2020.

15   Ibid.

16   Ibid.

17   Ibid.

18   Ibid.

19   Ibid.

20   Ibid.

21   Thomas Graziani, "Douyin, Kuaishou, Red, Bilibili: Where to Promote Your Brand in China Besides WeChat," Jing Daily, May 14, 2020. Web. https://jingdaily.com/douyin-kuaishou-red-bilibili-where-to-promote-your-brand-in-china-besides-wechat/

22   Tristan Rose, "How Does TikTok Make Money?," entrepreneur-360.com, April 8, 2022. Web. https://entrepreneur-360.com/how-does-tiktok-make-money-12356

23   Sara Lebow, "TikTok and Douyin Will Account for More Than 5% of Global Digital Ad Spend This Year," EMarketer.com, April 13, 2022. Web. https://emarketer.com/content/tiktok-douyin-digital-ad-spend

24   Michael Brennan, Attention Factory, Independently Published, October 10, 2020.

25   Emma Lee, "Douyin Sees Ecommerce Sales More Than Tripled in the Past Year," Technode.com, June 1, 2022. Web. https://technode.

com/2022/06/01/douyin-sees-e-commerce-sales-more-than-tripled-in-the-past-year/

26   Palash Ghosh, "Pinduoduo Is Now China's Biggest E-Commerce Platform As Billionaire Chairman Colin Huang Steps Down," Forbes, March 17, 2021, Web. https://www.forbes.com/sites/palashghosh/2021/03/17/pinduoduo-is-now-chinas-biggest-e-commerce-platform-as-billionaire-chairman-colin-huang-steps-down/?sh=45f8d6ae62b1

27   Elad Natanson, "The Miraculous Rise of Pinduoduo and its Lessons," Forbes, December 4, 2019, Web. https://www.forbes.com/sites/eladnatanson/2019/12/04/the-miraculous-rise-of-pinduoduo-and-its-lessons/?sh=fb51a11f1300

28   Ibid.

29   Kirk Enbysk, "How Pinduoduo Became the #2 eCommerce Marketplace in China," ApplicoInc, 2018, Web. https://www.applicoinc.com/blog/how-pinduoduo-became-the-2-ecommerce-marketplace-in-china/#:~:text=Pinduoduo%20is%20the%20fastest%2Dgrowing,years%2C%20respectively%2C%20to%20accomplish.

30   Companies Market Cap, Pinduoduo, April 2022, Web. https://companiesmarketcap.com/pinduoduo/marketcap/

31   Zihao Liu, "Is Xiaohongshu Losing Steam?" Jing Daily, January 4, 2022. Web. https://jingdaily.com/is-xiaohongshu-losing-steam/

32   News Wire "China's Xiaohongshu raises $500 mln, valuation hits $20 bln," Reuters, November 8, 2021.

33   Forbes Global 2000 List, Forbes, Accessed July 23, 2022. Web. https://www.forbes.com/lists/global2000

34   Xiao Hong Shu Press Room, "Our New Content to Commerce System," September 10, 2021, Web. https://www.xiaohongshu.com/en/newsroom/detail/empowering-small-businesses-with-our-new-content-to-commerce-system

35   Ibid.

36   V. Kasturi Rangan, Daniel Corsten, et al., "How Direct-to-Consumer Brands Can Continue to Grow," Harvard Business Review Magazine, November – December 2021 issue.

37   The 48th Statistical Report on the Development of China's Internet

Network, China Internet Information Center (CNNIC), December 2022.

38 Sophie Yu, Scott Murdoch, "'All girls, buy it!' In China, Perfect Diary gives cosmetics world a makeover with live streams, low prices," Reuters, August 26, 202, Web. https://www.reuters.com/article/us-china-cosmetics-perfectdiary/all-girls-buy-it-in-china-perfect-diary-gives-cosmetics-world-a-makeover-with-live-streams-low-prices-idUSKBN25M0BP

39 Shunyang Zhang, Sunil Gupta, "Perfect Diary" Case Study, Harvard Business School, August 20, 2021.

40 Editor, "Perfect Diary Case Study: How this Chinese Makeup Brand Got to the Top," Daxue Consulting, March 7, 2021, Web. https://daxueconsulting.com/perfect-diary-case-study-how-this-chinese-makeup-brand-got-to-the-top

41 Lawrence Nga, "Hillhouse backed Yatsen is Now Public. Here's What Investors Should Know," The Motley Fool, December 2, 2020, Web. https://www.fool.com/investing/2020/12/02/hillhouse-backed-cosmetics-company-yatsen-ipo/

42 Shunyang Zhang, Sunil Gupta, "Perfect Diary" Case Study, Harvard Business School, August 20, 2021.

43 Ibid.

44 Ibid.

45 Ibid.

46 Editor, "Perfect Diary Case Study: How this Chinese Makeup Brand Got to the Top," Daxue Consulting, March 7, 2021, Web. https://daxueconsulting.com/perfect-diary-case-study-how-this-chinese-makeup-brand-got-to-the-top

47 Shunyang Zhang, Sunil Gupta, "Perfect Diary" Case Study, Harvard Business School, August 20, 2021.

48 Ibid.

49 Lou Qiqin, "Obsessed by Products: A Look Inside Huang Jinfeng's Perfect Diary," Interview with Jinfeng Huang, Jiemian Global, November 30, 2021, Web. https://en.jiemian.com/article/6862046.html

50 Tech Buzz China by Pandaily Podcast, Episode 84, interview with Gary Liu, CEO, South China Morning Post, January 14, 2021.

51 Daxue Consulting, Perfect Diary Case Study, "How This Chinese Makeup Brand Got to the Top," March 7, 2021, Web. https://daxueconsulting.com/perfect-diary-case-study-how-this-chinese-makeup-brand-got-to-the-top/

52 Lawrence Nga, "Hillhouse backed Yatsen is Now Public. Here's What Investors Should Know," The Motley Fool, December 2, 2020, Web. https://www.fool.com/investing/2020/12/02/hillhouse-backed-cosmetics-company-yatsen-ipo/

53 Julienna Law, "Can Perfect Diary Take C-Beauty Global?," Jing Daily, July 20, 2021, Web. https://jingdaily.com/perfect-diary-c-beauty-global-expansion/

54 Ching Li Tor, "Perfect Diary's Parent Company Yatsen Lists on the US Stock Market," Beauty Tech Japan, medium.com, February 2, 2021. Web. https://medium.com/beautytech-jp/perfect-diarys-parent-company-yatsen-lists-on-the-us-stock-market-here-s-a-look-back-at-its-bc83957c35b1

55 AJ Cortese, "Beverage Unicorn Genki Forest Wants to be Treated Like a Tech Startup, but Does the Label Stick?" kr-asia.com, April 15, 2021, Web. https://kr-asia.com/beverage-unicorn-genki-forest-wants-to-be-treated-like-a-tech-startup-but-does-the-label-stick

56 Rui Ma, "Data Driven Iteration Helped China's Genki Forest Become a $6B Beverage Giant in 5 Years," TechCrunch, July 26, 2021. Web. https://techcrunch.com/2021/07/25/data-driven-iteration-helped-chinas-genki-forest-become-a-6b-beverage-giant-in-5-years/#:~:text=The%20bottled%20beverage%20industry%20wasn,outfit%20known%20as%20ELEX%20Technology.

57 Daiane Chen, "SHEIN Market Strategy: How the Chinese Fashion Brand is Conquering the West," Daxue Consulting, February 16, 2022. Web. https://daxueconsulting.com/shein-market-strategy/

58 Greg Petro, "The Future Of Fashion Retailing: The Zara Approach (Part 2 of 3)," Forbes, October 25, 2012. https://www.forbes.com/sites/gregpetro/2012/10/25/the-future-of-fashion-retailing-the-zara-approach-part-2-of-3/?sh=f2c67e67aa4b

59 Hueling Tan, "China Lipstick King Sold 1.7 Billion in Stuff in 12 Hours," Business Insider, October, 22, 2021. Web. https://www.businessinsider.com/china-lipstick-king-sold-17-billion-stuff-in-12-hours-2021-10

60 Ibid.

NOTES

61 Mandy Zuo, "Chines Heartthrob Deng Lun's Career in Limbo", South China Morning Post, March 16, 2022. Web. https://www.scmp.com/news/people-culture/china-personalities/article/3170685/chinese-heartthrob-deng-luns-career-limbo

62 Reuters, "China Tells Celebrities, Livestreamers to Report Tax Related Crimes by 2022", NBC News, December 22, 2021. Web. https://www.nbcnews.com/news/world/china-tells-celebrities-livestreamers-report-tax-related-crimes-2022-rcna9616

63 Cheryl Teh, "China is Tempting Customers with Its Flawless AI Influencers", Insider, August 13, 2021. Web. https://www.insider.com/chinas-flawless-ai-influencers-the-hot-new-queens-of-advertising-2021-8

64 Ibid.

65 Time Staff, "The 25 Most Influential People on the Internet," Time Magazine, June 30, 2018, Web. https://time.com/5324130/most-influential-internet/

66 Elizabeth Harris, "The 19-year-old is a Singer, a Model and an Influencer, Who is Worth $6M. What is the Miquela Phenomenon?" Agora Digital, March 29, 2020, Web. https://agoradigital.art/blog-who-is-miquela-sousa/#:~:text=The%2019%2Dyear%2Dold%20is,What%20is%20the%20Miquela's%20phenomenon%3F

67 Deborah Weinswig, "Alibaba's New Retail Integrates Ecommerce, Stores and Logistics: Is This the Next Gen of Retail?" Forbes, April 14, 2017, Web. https://www.forbes.com/sites/deborahweinswig/2017/04/14/alibabas-new-retail-integrates-e-commerce-stores-logistics-is-this-the-next-gen-of-retail/?sh=69b6ad8767c6

68 Wengshou Cui, "Hema: New Retail Comes to Grocery," International Institute for Management Case Study, Lausanne, Switzerland, 2019.

69 Ibid.

70 Glenn Taylor, "Alibaba Supermarkets Blend Offline and Online Via Mobile-First Strategy," Retail Touchpoints Magazine, July 26, 2017, Web. https://www.retailtouchpoints.com/topics/omnichannel-alignment/alibaba-supermarkets-blend-online-and-offline-via-mobile-first-strategy

71 Ibid.

72 Wengshou Cui, "Hema: New Retail Comes to Grocery," International Institute for Management Case Study, Lausanne, Switzerland, 2019.

73 Ibid.

74 Jing, Zang, "Hema Becomes China's Largest Retailer for Ready-to-Eat Avocados," Product Report, December 22, 2021, Web. https://www.producereport.com/article/hema-becomes-chinas-largest-retail-er-ready-eat-avocados

75 Bloomberg News Wire, "Alibaba's Fresh Hippo Said to Mull Funding at $10 Billion Value," bloomberg.com, Web. https://www.bloomberg.com/news/articles/2022-01-14/alibaba-s-freshippo-said-to-mull-funding-at-10-billion-value#xj4y7vzkg

76 Mark Tanner, "Online Delivery in China is Nothing Short of Gobsmacking," China Skinny, June 9, 2021, Web. https://www.chinaskinny.com/blog/online-delivery-china?utm_source=news_chinaskinny_com&utm_medium=email&utm_content=The+Weekly+China+Skinny&utm_campaign=20210608_m163525755_20210609+-+3&utm_term=View+on+the+web

77 Monica Suk, "Alibaba Deploys 1,000 Delivery Robots As E-Commerce Booms in China; Accelerates Digitization of Hainan," Alizilla (Alibaba Press Release), June 11, 2021, Web. https://www.alizila.com/alibaba-deploys-1000-delivery-robots-as-e-commerce-booms-in-china-accelerates-digitization-of-hainan/

78 Bloomberg News Wire, "Yum China's Bet on AI and Robot Servers is Beginning to Pay Off," March 5, 2019, Web. https://www.bloomberg.com/news/articles/2019-03-05/kfc-owner-defies-china-slowdown-with-a-i-menus-and-robot-servers

79 Ibid.

80 Press Release, "Yum China Named to Fast Company's Annual List of the World's Most Innovative Companies for 2020," Yum China, March 11, 2020, Web. https://ir.yumchina.com/news-releases/news-release-details/yum-china-named-fast-companys-annual-list-worlds-most-innovative

81 Yum China Net Income 2015-2021, MacroTrends, accessed April 2022. Web. https://www.macrotrends.net/stocks/charts/YUMC/yum-china-holdings/net-income

82 Ibid.

83 Barbara Ortutay, "Elon Musk Wants to Offer Americans an 'Everything App' Like China's WeChat," Fortune, October 15, 2022, Web. https://

fortune.com/2022/10/15/elon-musk-twitter-everything-app-x-wechat-america-china/

84 China Internet Watch Report, "WeChat Users and Platform Insights 2022," May 18, 2022. Web. https://www.chinainternetwatch.com/31608/wechat-statistics/

85 Julian Birkinshaw, Dickie Liang-Hong Ke, Enrique de Diego, "Innovation and Agility at Tencent's WeChat," Case Study, London Business School, August 2019.

86 Ibid.

87 Ibid.

88 Ibid.

89 Ibid.

90 Ibid.

91 Tingyi Chen, "The Top 500 WeChat Official Accounts," Walk the Chat Trend Report, June 11, 2017, Web. https://walkthechat.com/trend-report-top-500-wechat-official-account/

92 Julian Birkinshaw, Dickie Liang-Hong Ke, Enrique de Diego, "Innovation and Agility at Tencent's WeChat," Case Study, London Business School, August 2019.

93 Ibid.

94 Ibid.

95 Julian Birkinshaw, Dickie Liang-Hong Ke, Enrique de Diego, "The Kind of Creative Thinking That Fueled WeChat's Success," Harvard Business Review, October 29, 2019, Web. https://hbr.org/2019/10/the-kind-of-creative-thinking-that-fueled-wechats-success

96 Zhenpeng Huang, Sarah Zheng, "WeChat App Keeps Growing Despite Beijing Crackdown," Bloomberg, January 6, 2022. Web. https://www.bloomberg.com/news/articles/2022-01-06/tencent-s-wechat-app-keeps-growing-despite-beijing-crackdown

97 Ibid.

98 Ibid.

99 Ibid.

100 Ibid.

101 Tencent Press Release, "Tencent's WeCom Sees User Growth Amid Capabilities Integration With Other Tencent Platforms", January 14, 2022, Web. https://www.tencent.com/en-us/articles/2201273.html

102 Roel Wieringa, Jaap Gordijn, "The Business Models of WeChat," The Value Engineers white paper, March 2021.

103 Feiran Lu, "Grandma is Dead. So How is She Stoll Talking to Us?" SHINE News, April 7, 2023, Web. https://www.shine.cn/news/in-focus/2304076307/

104 Tyler Xie, "Innovating the 'On-Demand' Creative Economy with Tezign Founder and CEO Dr. Fan Ling," The Harbinger China, November 2, 2017, Web. https://medium.com/the-harbinger-china

105 Ibid.

106 Doris Yu, "Temasek, SoftBank invest in Sequoia-backed Chinese Marketing Solutions Start-up," techinasia.com, March 18, 2021, Web. https://www.techinasia.com/temasek-softbank-invest-sequoia-backed-chinese-marketing-solutions-startup-tezign

107 NetDragon Financial Statements, 2020, released March 2021, Web. http://ir.nd.com.cn/en/

108 ABP News Bureau, "Chinese Gaming Firm Appoints AI Robot as CEO, Sees 10 Percent Growth in Share Price," March 17, 2023, Web. https://news.abplive.com/technology/chinese-gaming-firm-netdragon-websoft-appoints-ai-robot-as-ceo-sees-10-percent-growth-in-share-price-1589029

109 Turing Test, Stanford Encyclopedia of Philosophy, First published Wed Apr 9, 2003; substantive revision Mon Oct 4, 2021, Web. https://plato.stanford.edu/entries/turing-test/

About the Author

Award-winning CEO Joanna Hutchins has spent the last 15 years empowering global consumer brands and Fortune 500 companies to innovate and expand their strategies. Her career in brands and marketing has been vast, beginning in New York City where she won multiple Effie Awards from the American Marketing Association (AMA) for her cutting-edge campaigns. She then moved to Bangkok, Singapore, and finally Shanghai, where she has been based since 2010. Joanna is the author of *Chinafy: Why China is leading the West in innovation and how the rest of the world can catch up* (2023).

Accolades: "China's 50 Top Marketing Leaders" (New Internationalist); "Business Leader of the Year" (International Professional Women's Society); "CEO of the Year" (shortlisted; Campaign Asia's Women Leading Change Awards)